Melinda Listerud

END TIMES

Psalm 27:4

Other Books by Clyne W. Buxton

Expect These Things

This Way to Better Teaching

What About Tomorrow?

Minister's Service Manual

END TIMES

A Biblical Study of Current and Future Events

Clyne W. Buxton

CLEVELAND, TENNESSEE 37311

First Printing   December 1993

Second Printing   February 1995

Unless otherwise noted all Scripture quotations are from *the Holy Bible, New International Version.* Copyright © 1973, 1978, 1984 by International Bible Society. Used by permission of Zondervan Bible Publishers.

Library of Congress Catalog Card Number: 93-086125

ISBN Number: 0871482932

Copyright © 1993 by Pathway Press

Cleveland, Tennessee 37311

All Rights Reserved

Printed in the United States of America

*To Valerie, Jonathan, and David,
all of whom are a source
of pride and joy to their
grandparents, who pray daily
that as they develop in stature,
they will also mature in Christ.*

Contents

1. Times of the End 9
2. Middle East, Key to End Times 21
3. God's Prophetic Word 33
4. Money and Last Days 43
5. The Rapture 53
6. The Judgment of Believers 73
7. The World After the Rapture 87
8. The Great Tribulation 111
9. The Earthly Reign of Christ 129
   God's Plan of World Events Chart 150
   Bibliography 151

CHAPTER 1

TIMES of the END

Why should we believe these are the last days? History shows that at the close of other centuries there have been prophets of doom proclaiming that the end was imminent. Are we hearing such prophets today just because the 20th century is ending and some men think the worst of the uncharted future? The cardinal question is, do we have unequivocal biblical proof that these are indeed the end times? The thesis of this book is that we have abundant proof from the Bible showing that the end may be very near.

Numerous prophetic references which have lain dormant for millennia have been fulfilled within recent times. Shadows of awesome events to come upon mankind after the Rapture fall long across our paths today. Even some Bible students not easily alarmed wonder if the present age might cease before the end of the century.

Why the concern about these times being the last days?

END TIMES

Simply because all about us the groundwork for the fulfillment of the escatological predictions of the end times is being laid. Following are a few examples. Only recently could a worldwide numbering system foretold in Revelation 13:16 be carried out, thanks to the computer. A world government predicted in Daniel 7:23 and Revelation 13:7 is now being openly discussed by prominent world leaders. The founding of the United Nations in 1946 may have been the first step toward such a world government.

Not until recently has any country on earth ever been able to muster an army of 200 million soldiers in fulfillment of Revelation 9:16. Mao Tse-tung, late ruler of China, boasted in his diary that he could have a 200 million-man army. The Bible foretells such an army marching on Palestine at Armageddon, the climactic end of this age.

The Book of Revelation predicts that the Euphrates River will be dried up so that armies of the East may cross enroute to the Battle of Armageddon (Revelation 16:12). It appears that recent developments in Turkey have set the stage for this end-time reference to be fulfilled. The January 13, 1990, *Indianapolis Star* carried a news article with the headline "Turkey Will Cut Off Flow of Euphrates for One Month."

The article said that Turkey had built a huge reservoir capable of containing a month's flow of the river. By diverting the Euphrates channel, the river bed below the reservoir may be dried up at will. It seems that with this new dam, now completed, Turkey has the ability to stop the flow of the mighty Euphrates at any time. The conditions for fulfilling the ancient prophecy about stopping the river appear to be in place.

Add to these staggering facts the spectacular fulfillment of numerous prophecies of Israel's return to Palestine (see

Isaiah 11:11, 12; Jeremiah 33:25, 26; Ezekiel 37:21, 25; Romans 11:26, 27), the founding of the European Economic Community (Daniel 7:7, 24; Revelation 13:1; 17:3, 12, 13), and Daniel's prediction of peace in Israel immediately following the Rapture (Daniel 9:27).

Dormant Prophecies Fulfilled

It is most significant that all of these prophecies had lain dormant for hundreds upon hundreds of years. Now, one after the other, awesome prophecies are being fulfilled before our eyes. Since the Bible is clear to point out that these things would come to pass at the end of the Gentile age, we know that we are living in the times of the end.

The very term *end times* implies a cessation of human history as we know it. However, whenever we speak of the end, we do not necessarily mean the end of the world—though the Bible predicts that ultimately the world will end, or be renovated and made anew. Instead, we usually use the term end times to refer to an age that will close with cataclysmic upheaval, with the Battle of Armageddon, and with the return of Christ to earth. Then the Gentile age will end. A tranquil 1,000-year reign of Christ upon earth will follow.

Until now, no generation since Christ has had such overwhelming reason to believe that it is the last to live on earth before the Lord's return. Every major world event that happens today seems to move us closer to the ultimate confrontation between Christ and Satan, which the Bible says will follow the Rapture.

In his book *Approaching Hoofbeats: the Four Horsemen of the Apocalypse*, Billy Graham commented, "There is something ominous in the air, and my bones . . . vibrate with the horror and hope of it." Graham continued, "Everywhere I go I find people, both leaders and ordinary individuals, asking one basic question, 'Is there any hope?' And the answer comes roaring back from the world's press: 'There is no hope for planet Earth!'"

Our Hope in Turbulent Days

We know, however, that such a sentiment is wrong. In Christ there is hope, abundant hope; and it is resident in the saving and keeping faith of Jesus Christ. However, pity the person whose faith is not in Christ; his future is hopeless indeed until he turns to the Lord.

Though the Bible gives guidelines for living in these turbulent times, too many individuals seek answers to the world's dilemma outside God's Word. In his work *Global Peace*, Dave Hunt reminds us, "Many Christians have written the topic off [doctrine of last days] as a scare tactic employed by sensationalist evangelists when all else has failed to 'awaken the sinners.' And there are those, both Christians and non-Christians, who angrily denounce any talk about the 'last days' as negative gloom-and-doom defeatism that breeds pessimism and holds back progress."

Later Hunt insists, "It is certainly legitimate to attempt to understand how near we may be to our Lord's second coming by examining current events for the 'last days signs' which the Bible offers." Hunt is on target in suggesting that we examine the Holy Scriptures. In doing so, we learn that contemporary developments point to imminent destructive upheaval, which both the Old and New Testaments foretell.

The Coming Mark of the Beast

Revelation 13 warns of a time when mankind may not

buy or sell without having an identifying mark in the hand or forehead. The mark requirement will be a universal law set up by a ruthless world leader whom the Bible calls Antichrist. Not until the last few years could such a decree be carried out on a global basis. Only recently has technology developed computers, communication satellites, and worldwide banking networks sufficient to enforce such a law.

A friend of the author, a church official in Europe, says that today in France a "mark" such as the one described in Revelation is in use as an experiment. Some banks there have installed a computerized system so that the cost of merchandise may be electronically deducted from a customer's bank account. Upon making a purchase in a store, the customer passes a marking on the back of his hand over a light. This sets machines in motion, telling the bank computers to deduct the amount of the purchase from the customer's account. No checks, no cash, no credit cards needed! Convenient, isn't it?

Never has the mark of the Beast been so accessible, so practical, and so near! Do any of us doubt that the French practice is a carbon copy of the Revelation prediction? Can we not see that this is a clear sign of the end times? The procedure in France is not the mark of the Beast, but it is a chilling forerunner of it.

Look closely at the following Revelation prediction, referring to the world ruler who will lead a world government:

> He also forced everyone, small and great, rich and poor, free and slave, to receive a mark on his right hand or on his forehead, so that no one could buy or sell unless he had the mark, which is the name of the beast or the number of his name. . . . A third angel

followed them and said in a loud voice: "If anyone worships the beast and his image and receives his mark on the forehead or on the hand, he, too, will drink of the wine of God's fury, which has been poured full strength into the cup of his wrath. He will be tormented with burning sulfur in the presence of the holy angels and of the Lamb. And the smoke of their torment rises for ever and ever. There is no rest day or night for those who worship the beast and his image, or for anyone who receives the mark of his name" (Revelation 13:16, 17; 14:9-11).

There are many other end-time signs besides the nearness of the mark of the Beast, but that sign is important. For example, it appears that the computer, a fairly recent development of technology, will implement the mark. Larry W. Poland has an interesting comment on the subject. Writing in *How to Prepare for the Coming Persecution*, he says, "You must have stood helplessly and endlessly in line with other computer-age refugees at a major store because their computers were down. You must have found yourself blushing in the front of a checkout line—unable to buy or sell—because some mysterious little machine told the cashier the 'mark' of your credit card was not acceptable."

Poland continues: "My bank manager friend with Bank of America tells me that all their managers have been briefed on the advent of totally cashless economics—societies in which all financial transactions are electronic transfers by computer. He tells me their briefings included reference to the mega-computer in Belgium that will tie all world finance together. They call it—get this—the Beast."

Nearness of the End

Not only does the ominous sign of the mark of the Beast loom high on the horizon, but many other end-time events appear to be very near also. Following is a list of major developments of the future foretold in the Bible. Note how close our generation is to most of them.

1. *Rapture.* All scriptures are fulfilled; Christ could come at any time now (1 Corinthians 15:51-55; 1 Thessalonians 4:13-18).

2. *Ten-Nation Confederacy.* The European Economic Community, very active today, seems to fulfill this prediction, especially if it ultimately contains 10 strong nations (Daniel 7:7, 24; Revelation 13:1; 17:3, 12, 13).

3. *Rise of world ruler.* He is not known today in that capacity, but he may be alive awaiting his cue from Satan after the Rapture (Daniel 7:8; 9:27; Revelation 13:1-8).

4. *Treaty bringing peace to Israel.* Such a treaty is being discussed at this writing (Daniel 9:27; Matthew 24:15, 16).

5. *Russia destroyed in Israel.* Whatever the country's ultimate formation, we know that Ezekiel's prediction will be fulfilled (Ezekiel 38; 39).

6. *World church active.* The World Council of Churches began in 1948, and the world church may develop from it. This end-time religious system will be active the first half of the Tribulation but will be destroyed by Antichrist (Revelation 17:1-18).

7. *Treaty with Israel broken.* This act ushers in the last half of Tribulation period, called Great Tribulation (Daniel 7:23; 9:27; Matthew 24:21, 22; Revelation 13:5-8).

8. *Satan worship.* This practice will become the worldwide state religion (Revelation 13:4, 8, 12, 15).

9. *Devastating judgments upon earth.* These include the seal judgments, trumpet judgments, and vial judgments (Revelation 6; 8; 9; 16).

10. *Battle of Armageddon.* This will be a world war in the Middle East (Revelation 9:13-21; 16:12-16).

11. *Second coming of Christ.* Christ will end the Battle of Armageddon (Matthew 24:27-31; Revelation 19:11-21).

12. *Satan bound.* This will be for a period of 1,000 years (Revelation 20:1-3).

13. *Deceased tribulation saints—and possibly Old Testament saints—resurrected* (Daniel 12:2; Revelation 20:4).

14. *Christ reigns.* Christ will set up His righteous rule on earth for a millennium (Revelation 20:5, 6).

15. *Great White Throne Judgment.* All wicked dead since Adam will be judged (Revelation 20:11-15).

16. *New heaven, new earth, eternity* (Revelation 21; 22).

A sure sign that this age is drawing to a close is that events predicted to take place after the Rapture are already developing—awaiting fruition just after the church departs. Should Christ come today, all of the events listed above through the Second Coming (number 11) would transpire within the next seven years.

Justification of the Tribulation

Most of us are optimists, and it is not easy for some of us to believe that such catastrophe awaits the world. Nonetheless, that is exactly what God's Word foretells. How could a loving God allow worldwide suffering and destruction? Why would He permit the dreadful Tribulation to come?

On the other hand, a holy God whose very nature is purity and righteousness must surely ask how much longer can He allow wicked man to mock Him with gross sins and flagrant dishonor of His Son. God will allow the Tribulation in order to bring unregenerate man to the end of himself and to bring mankind to its knees so that some will repent and be saved. He will allow the holocaust upon the earth to show His power, to demonstrate that He is the sovereign God.

In his book *Will Man Survive*? J. Dwight Pentecost, anticipating the imminent Tribulation, wrote: "It seems as though God has prepared this world for judgment. In spite of the generations of preaching and teaching and warning, men have rejected the message of the Word of God and it appears that God is bringing them now to the time of judgment. The only thing that prevents the beginning of that judgment is the presence of the believers here on earth now. The time could shortly come when the stage master will push the button and the curtain will go up, and those judgments will begin."

The unbeliever should be concerned about these times. In *Approaching Hoofbeats*, Billy Graham observes, "If I were not a believer in Christ, I might at this point in history succumb to total pessimism." The evangelist continues, "Ellen Goodman wrote in her column that 'With Armageddon perhaps around the corner, what are intelligent people to do? Wrap ourselves in mourning sheets and wait for the end?'"

No, we are not to pull mourning sheets about us nor wallow in despair. Rather, our security and hope is in Christ Jesus. The old hymn reminds us, "On Christ, the solid Rock, I stand; all other ground is sinking sand."

Worldwide Concern

The unregenerate are worried. The secular press often uses terms like *apocalypse* and *Armageddon*, both of which refer to catastrophe and the last days. Speaking of our reaction to last-day events, Charles H. Dyer says in *The Rise of Babylon*, "As we watch events in the Middle East unfold, it appears that these [end-time] events could occur soon. What then ought to be our response? Your response depends on where you stand in relationship to God. God has stated plainly in the Bible that His ultimate desire for mankind is eternal life—life to the fullest both now and in eternity to come."

Naturally, we are all concerned about the dark clouds of the last days which loom on the horizon. We should be even more concerned, however, about the end of our individual earthly lives. If Christ tarries, we are all going to die. Certainly, if we are not ready for death, we are not ready for the Rapture. As the apostle Peter admonished, "Be even more diligent to make your calling and election sure" (2 Peter 1:10, *NKJV*). The prerequisite for going in the Rapture is the same as for going to heaven by death. In either case we must be "in Christ"—His blood must cover our sins. We must know Him as Savior and Lord.

Awful, devastating events are ahead. Christ said the times will be so destructive that unless they were stopped, no flesh could survive. Only in recent years has man acquired the ability, with the help of nuclear weapons, to destroy the entire population of the earth. Bows and arrows, swords and spears of another age could not have wiped out all life. It is even doubtful that the conventional weapons of World War II could have done so. However, it is no longer difficult to fathom that contemporary man could completely destroy everything that breathes.

Redemption Is Near

Though the future may look dismal, Christ taught that we should not worry during the end times. His Olivet

Discourse, found in all three synoptic Gospels, is generally understood to deal with times of the end. Our Lord said, "Make up your mind not to worry beforehand how you will defend yourselves. For I will give you words and wisdom that none of your adversaries will be able to resist or contradict" (Luke 21:14, 15).

Again, still speaking of these last days, Jesus said, "When these things begin to take place, stand up and lift up your heads, because your redemption is drawing near" (Luke 21:28).

Actually, these are not days of utter hopelessness, and we are to constantly tell our unconverted friends that fact. Christ is still the Prince of Peace. Our future is as bright as the promises of God. These days offer unprecedented opportunities for us to walk hand in hand with God as we see the predictions of Scripture being fulfilled. These times also offer tremendous opportunities to witness to the unconverted, using end-time events as a backdrop. Let us rejoice because God has taken us into His confidence, showing us in His Word what lies ahead. Remember, Christ told us to stand up and lift up our heads as the end approaches.

MIDDLE EAST, KEY to END TIMES

Recorded history began in the Middle East; and according to the Bible, history as we know it will end there. Though man's origin dates earlier, recorded history began about 3300 B.C. with the Sumerians who lived between the Euphrates and Tigris Rivers in what is now Iraq. Their homeland, called *Mesopotamia*, which means "land between the rivers," was of great historical significance.

The Sumerians invented writing, a cornerstone of civilization. They also invented the wheel, adopted the 60-minute hour, and wrote a code of laws, many of which are still used by modern man. This area, part of the Fertile Crescent, was the home of the Tower of Babel, Nineveh, Babylon, and apparently Noah and the Ark. Also the Garden of Eden is believed to have been there; so was Ur, the home of Abraham. Daniel and Ezekiel wrote their prophetic books in that area, and the Jews were held captive there for 70 years. Apparently, an early Christian church was located in the vicinity, for Peter wrote, "The church at Babylon salutes you" (1 Peter 5:13, KJV). Of course, modern Iraq, site of ancient civilization, is only one of numerous countries in that part of the world.

Hub of Three Continents

The term *Middle East* in modern usage is applied to the lands around the eastern end of the Mediterranean Sea. Strictly speaking, the designation includes such countries as Libya, Greece, and Turkey, among others; but usually when we speak of the Middle East, we have in mind Syria, Lebanon, Israel, Jordan, Egypt, Saudi Arabia, Kuwait, Iraq, and Iran.

Most of these are poor countries, comprised of arid lands, rocky mountainsides, and in some parts vast sand dunes. Nonbelievers have had difficulty in the past accepting the biblical prediction that a world war would someday be fought in the region. They could not believe the land was worth fighting for—but that was before the advent of the importance of crude oil, a bountiful commodity of the Middle East.

War strategists used to say that armies of the world moved on their bellies, meaning they had to have adequate food. Today armies move on the fuel tank. Without oil, no plane flies, no missile is fired, no tank moves, and most ships stay in port. The world has to have oil to survive. The Middle East has nearly two-thirds of the world's oil supply, and that fact catapults the area to centerstage in world importance. Oil also gives the Middle East central significance in prophecy, making the area the centerpiece of world destiny. Therefore, the entire world has a vital interest in developments in the Middle East.

Importance of Oil

The power of the Middle East became obvious in 1973. At that time the United States refused to support Saudi Arabia against Israel, so Saudi Arabia cut off our oil supply. Within a few weeks automobiles lined up at the gas pumps, seeking gasoline at ever-increasing prices. The economy of America was greatly affected, inflation increased rapidly, and the price of gasoline, or anything else, has not been the same since. We consume 39 percent of the world's annual oil production, and without it our economy would collapse.

Most of the rest of the world depends on Middle Eastern oil also. For example, if the 1973 oil embargo had lasted six to nine months longer, it would have destroyed the economy of both Japan and Europe. The fact is, the entire world economy depends on a steady flow of oil. That point makes the Middle East the most important area in the world, for it has most of the earth's oil reserves.

In his work, *Armageddon, Oil and the Middle East Crisis*, John F. Walvoord says, "It will be in the Middle East that the future world government will have its base of political and economic power. The enigma of how the undeveloped Middle East could ever become the center of world history again has suddenly been solved by the tremendous wealth and power latent in the oil reserves of the area. Already strategic geographically as the hub of three continents, the Middle East is destined in the future to take a leading role in international and business affairs."

The National Geographic Society has estimated most of the world's oil reserves as follows:

Middle East

Saudi Arabia	258 billion barrels
Iraq	100 billion barrels
United Arab Emirates	98 billion barrels
Kuwait	97 billion barrels
Iran	93 billion barrels
Egypt	5 billion barrels
Syria	2 billion barrels

Remainder of World

Venezuela	59 billion barrels
USSR (formerly)	58 billion barrels
Mexico	56 billion barrels
United States	26 billion barrels
China	24 billion barrels

Note that those fairly small and seemingly insignificant Middle Eastern countries suddenly find themselves capable of manipulating world economy by controlling the oil supply. Those seven countries hold 653 billion barrels of oil in reserve, while the rest of the entire world has only 223 billion barrels, or only about one-third of the total. Remember, the United States consumes more than one-third of the world's annual production.

The Holy Spirit knew all about the oil reserves and the part they would play in end-time events. Therefore, He moved upon the prophets to foretell that the Middle East would become the hub of world events; that Israel would be attacked in the climactic battle called Armageddon; that the Euphrates River, discussed twice in Revelation, would play

a part in end times; and that the great world war—
Armageddon—would be fought in the Middle East.

Israel, the Pivotal Country

However, the Arab nations with all their financial clout are not nearly so important to the end times as another Middle Eastern country—the nation of Israel. The Bible foretells that Israel will ultimately triumph; that the nation will someday hold all the land east of Palestine to the Euphrates River; that Christ will rule the world for a thousand years from Jerusalem; and that the 12 apostles, then resurrected, will rule the 12 tribes of Israel in Palestine. How explicit God is about the future of the Middle East!

Today Israel's population comprises only about twice as many people as Moses led to the Promised Land millennia ago. However, the people and the land are important to future world events. Speaking of Israel's place at the end of the age, John Walvoord says, "In the center of the stage is the little nation Israel, insignificant in number among the billions of the world's population and yet the fuse for the final world conflict that is ahead."

Jerusalem is an ancient and well-known city of Israel. Though not large, the city has been better known through the centuries by more people than the name of any other city in the world.

According to prophetic scripture, God intends to bring about a thousand years of peace with a Jewish Messiah as the ruler, Jerusalem as the world capital, Israel as the chosen land, and the rest of the world under the peaceful dominion of the righteous Messiah. God's plans for the Jews and the Holy Land are everlasting. Throughout eternity the Jews will play an important part in God's economy. Even the 12 gates to the New Jerusalem will each bear the name of one of Jacob's sons (Revelation 21:12). Among all the peoples of the Middle East, none are as remarkable as the Jews.

Why is God so explicit concerning that race belonging to Him? Does He love the Jews more than the other races, which are also part of His creation? God's Word gives a clear answer to these questions in the call of Abraham thousands of years ago: "I will make you into a great nation and I will bless you; I will make your name great, and you will be a blessing. I will bless those who bless you, and whoever curses you I will curse; and all peoples on earth will be blessed through you" (Genesis 12:2, 3).

Why God Chose Israel

God elected and commissioned the Jews so that they in turn would be a spiritual blessing to the world. Ultimately "all peoples on earth" would be blessed through the Messiah who would redeem man and reign over him in peace.

Commenting on God's selection of Abraham, and through him the selection of the Jews, Henry Goerner, writing in his book *Thus It Is Written*, related: "God's choice of Abraham had an arbitrary element in it. This selection was not made on the basis of the inherent merit of the man, but on the assumption that he might prove usable for God's purpose. The descendants of Abraham were God's chosen people on the same basis." Therefore, except as they know and follow God's will, the Jews are no more holy, nor any more favored by God, nor any more excused for their sins, than any other race.

The promises made to Abraham were reconfirmed with Isaac (Genesis 26:2-5), with Jacob (Genesis 28:13-15), and at

Sinai with all of Israel. It was there that Moses said, "Because he loved your forefathers and chose their descendants after them, he brought you out of Egypt by his Presence and his great strength" (Deuteronomy 4:37).

Israel's national election is unconditional and perpetual; therefore, God will keep His covenant with the nation. Jehovah chose that people and taught the great principles of a holy life to them, and He showed them the way to eternal life. In this world of paganistic, Satan-dominated men, God needed a people He could set apart from the rest of mankind in order to teach His precepts to them.

Jehovah chose the Jews so that they might learn of Him and then reveal Him to the world, both by precept and example. In *Rebirth of the State of Israel*, Arthur W. Kac suggests: "There is only one sound and logical view by which to account for the indestructibility of the Jews. This view is set forth in the Bible where the survival of the Jews is attributed to the unchangeable will of God, and where the preservation of the Jews is part and parcel of their national destiny as a people chosen of God to fulfill a certain mission in the world."

God's Care During Dark Years

The Jews were scattered throughout the Old World after the Exile. This was known as the Diaspora (dispersion). The last group of Jews to be taken from Israel was by Nebuchadnezzar in 586 B.C. A little more than 100 years earlier, the 10 northern tribes had been removed from the Holy Land. For 70 retributive years, the Jews were exiled in Babylon, after which some of them returned to Israel. However, many Jews either stayed in Chaldea (Babylonia) or dispersed into other areas of the world rather than returning after the Exile.

The promises in God's prophetic Word are inspiring concerning Jehovah's interest in the Jews during their centuries of Diaspora. God himself said, "When they are in the land of their enemies, I will not reject them or abhor them so as to destroy them completely, breaking my covenant with them. I am the Lord their God" (Leviticus 26:44). Through Jeremiah He declared: "If I have not established my covenant with day and night and the fixed laws of heaven and earth, then I will reject the descendants of Jacob and David my servant and will not choose one of his sons to rule over the descendants of Abraham, Isaac and Jacob. For I will restore their fortunes and have compassion on them" (33:25, 26).

Just as Moses foretold, the Israelites were scattered "among all nations, from one end of the earth to the other" (Deuteronomy 28:64). He also predicted, "You will live in constant suspense, filled with dread both night and day, never sure of your life" (v. 66). None of us doubt the repeated fulfillment of this prophecy. The darkest pages of history have to do with the maltreatment of Jewish people. The nations have seen to it that the prophecy concerning the Jews found in verse 65 has come true: "You will find no repose, no resting place for the sole of your foot." It is true that some countries, especially the United States, have been kinder than others. However, even in this nation we have had our anti-Semitism.

In this century, Jews have been banished, tortured, and massacred more than in any other century in history. It is inconceivable that man in this "enlightened" age could be so barbaric. The Soviet Union as well as Hitler annihilated millions of Jews.

In spite of hatred, persecution, and mass murder, the Jews live on. They could paraphrase Tennyson's poem about the brook and sing, "Nations come and nations go, but we live on forever." Concerning the indestructibility of the Jews, Charles H. Stevens commented in *Prophecy and the Seventies*: "The enigma of history is the preservation of the sons of Jacob. There they stand singularly alone, magnificently different, defiantly unchanged. Like the Bible itself, the descendants of Abraham are standing like a Gibraltar, beat upon by a ceaseless and angry tide of hatred and opposition but still remaining the eternal nation."

Prophecy of the Return

The Bible clearly declares that the Jews were to return shortly before the Messiah comes to rule. They did so in 1948. Therefore, it appears evident that at any moment the following three stages, one following the other, could take place: (1) the return of Christ for the church (the Rapture); (2) the reign of the Antichrist for seven years (the Tribulation); (3) the return of Christ to the earth to end the battle of Armageddon and to set up His thousand-year reign (the Millennium).

Today the little Middle Eastern country of Israel is buzzing with activity. Already the desert is blossoming "as the rose" (Isaiah 35:1, KJV), and barren hillsides and mosquito-infested lowlands are giving way to bountiful yields season after season. The country exports food to Europe, technology to Japan, and flowers to Holland. Israel is one of only six countries in the world that has a surplus food supply. This fact is incredible when you remember that as late as 1948 the consensus of world opinion was that a people could hardly even survive there. This, too, is fulfillment of Scripture: "The desolate land will be cultivated instead of lying desolate in the sight of all who pass through it. They will say 'This land that was laid waste has become like the garden of Eden'" (Ezekiel 36:34, 35).

Many Orthodox Jews realize that they have returned under the guidance of God; and now they are intently asking Him to send the Messiah, not realizing that Jesus Christ is that promised Redeemer. The Reverend James E. Marks, a Jew converted to Christianity, writing in *The Church of God Evangel*, tells of a visit to the famed Wailing Wall, located in the old Temple area in Jerusalem: "Men were swaying back and forth with perspiration pouring from their faces; they were lost in worship to God. They were saying, 'I believe with perfect faith in the coming of the Messiah: and though he tarry, I will wait faithfully for his coming' [a daily prayer of the Jews]."

The Bible says that the Jews would return to the Middle East, Christ would translate the church, and then the Jews would undergo the Tribulation while in their homeland. In fact, the passages referring to that seven-year period are directed chiefly to God's elect, the Jews. Christ talks exclusively to the Israelites in the Olivet Discourse (Matthew 24). However, the Bible also reveals that the Tribulation will be upon all nations of the earth and will affect both Jew and Gentile. Jeremiah describes those days of Tribulation: "How awful that day will be! None will be like it. It will be a time of trouble for Jacob, but he will be saved out of it" (30:7).

When the Rapture takes the believers from the earth, that event will probably cause many Jews to rethink their stand concerning Jesus Christ, and some will turn to Him. The 144,000 Jewish evangelists will convert untold numbers of both Jews and Gentiles during the seven-year Tribulation.

Christ, Lord of the Jews

The Bible foretells a spiritual regeneration of the returning people. This is significant in light of the low spiritual condition of many Jews today. Though some of them may be cold, calculating, and godless, God has promised: "I will give you a new heart and put a new spirit in you; I will remove from you your heart of stone and give you a heart of flesh. And I will put my Spirit in you and move you to follow my decrees and be careful to keep my laws. You will live in the land I gave your forefathers; you will be my people, and I will be your God" (Ezekiel 36:26-28).

In the Scriptures time and again Israel's return to the land of the Book is connected with a return to the God of the Book. Jehovah promises to "change the speech of my returning people to pure Hebrew so that all can worship the Lord together" (Zephaniah 3:9, *TLB*). The small Middle Eastern country of Israel is now ripe for revival, for already pure Hebrew is the official speech throughout the land.

Someday Armageddon will be fought in the Holy Land, probably over oil. All of the oil-rich countries will be significant in end-time events. However, according to the Scriptures, none will be nearly so important as Israel. It will be from there that the holy Messiah will rule the earth in a thousand-year righteous reign of peace. May God speed that day!

GOD'S PROPHETIC WORD

As the world races toward the final hour of struggle known as Armageddon, we need to be alert to what the Bible says about these last days. Our God does speak clearly about the end times, and His holy predictions are as certain as the character of God himself. The developments of the world are rushing along, carefully following the script written by God from the beginning.

When speaking of His ability to foretell the future, God said, "Remember the former things, those of long ago; I am God, and there is no other; I am God, and there is none like me. I make known the end from the beginning, from ancient times, what is still to come. I say: My purpose will stand, and I will do all that I please" (Isaiah 46:9, 10). Nonetheless, many people shy away from God's prophetic Word, saying either it is too difficult or it is not important. We know that is not the case. All of the Bible was given as a guidebook for us to follow.

END TIMES

In his book *Global Peace*, Dave Hunt discusses the prospect of peace in the 1990s. Also, he deals with the importance of biblical prophecy: "Very few Christians have spent the time and effort necessary to understand, much less do they believe, *all* of the prophecy given to us in Scripture. No wonder so many church leaders in our day still overlook the criteria that so unequivocally determine the *timing* of Christ's return." Speaking of fulfillment of prophecy, Hunt said, "I have lived long enough to see much of what I learned in my youth as *prophecy* become *history*. It is awesome to watch events unfold in consummation of prophecies recorded in the Bible thousands of years ago. The most incredible events are yet to come, and the Bible has laid out the script for us in advance."

The unparalleled truths found in the Bible concerning our incredible future stagger our imagination. When we read of the Lord Jesus snatching the believers from the world, or of a one-man, worldwide rule in the person of the Antichrist during the Tribulation, or the thousand-year reign of Christ right here upon this old earth—these things appear farfetched and unbelievable to the natural mind. To expect such phenomenal happenings would qualify as extreme religious fanaticism if God's Word did not spell them out. But it does; and since we accept the Bible as God's book, we believe those things will come to pass.

Prophecy is "heady stuff," it has been said; and we may sometimes appear sensational, though not intentionally so, when speaking of things to come. However, some of the other cardinal doctrines of the Scriptures already fulfilled seemed sensational too. The virgin birth of our Lord, for example, once a part of predictive prophecy, was a phenomenal happening. Further, the very fact that the cold, lifeless body of Jesus came to life again was most certainly a supernatural event unbelievable to the natural mind. Likewise, the thought of Christ's coming again is incredible. Jehovah is a miracle-working God; and miracles, being completely out of the realm of ordinary things, are often nearly inconceivable to mortal man.

Nonetheless, God does not do things just to impress us or to be showy, and He would have us to proceed cautiously and to handle correctly the word of Truth (2 Timothy 2:15) when delving into the future. We should speak only where the Lord speaks.

The Lord knows what is ahead, and He has seen fit to reveal a good deal of the future to us. He told the apostle John, writer of the last book of the Bible, to set down three things: (1)"what you have seen," (2) "what is now," and (3) "what will take place later" (Revelation 1:19).

Though John did write of what he had seen and of the things that were, almost all of Revelation speaks of things yet to transpire. In fact, the entire book after chapter 3 is generally considered by Evangelical expositors to be futuristic.

Prophecy Overwhelms

The angel Gabriel appeared to Daniel and told him, "I am going to tell you what will happen later in the time of wrath, because the vision concerns the appointed time of the end" (Daniel 8:19). When Daniel was shown things to come, he was overwhelmed, just as we are. Verse 27 states that he "was exhausted and lay ill for several days."

More than 25 percent of the Bible was predictive when it was written, and to discount prophecy is to disavow over one-fourth of God's book. The Lord Jesus fully supported prophecy, for He said: "If you believed Moses, you would believe me, for he wrote about me" (John 5:46). And John wrote, "The testimony of Jesus is the spirit of prophecy" (Revelation 19:10). These references point out that Christ is the center of prophecy, just as He is the center of all Scripture.

The Lord looks at the end of things from the beginning, and He can speak of the future more easily than we can talk of history. About half of the prophetic Word is not yet fulfilled, and when one considers that we are quite probably living right at the close of this age, it is both exciting and sobering to realize that within the next few years much of prophecy could be fulfilled.

We do not have to be like Churchill, who wept as he mused on the awful unfolding of the future, for Jesus said, "When these things begin to take place, stand up and lift up your heads, because your redemption is drawing near" (Luke 21:28).

We can treat prophecy several ways: (1) We can ignore it; (2) we can teach nothing else but prophecy; or (3) we can teach the entire Bible, including prophecy. I am sure the last is God's way for us to deal with the future. Notwithstanding, many well-meaning people shy away from prophetic references altogether, honestly feeling that to be the best course for them.

A well-meaning friend of a minister said to him, "You had better stay out of Revelation. I notice those who read that book become foolish and cranky!" Speaking of prophecy in the book *God's Plan for the Future*, Lehman Strauss stated, "I believe it can be said, without fear of contradiction, that those who reject it know little or nothing about it. What a sad commentary on our church leaders, seminary leaders and pastors."

In passing over the prophetic truths concerning the

future, many people may be guilty of the same error the Jews committed when they discounted the more than 300 predictions in their sacred writings concerning the coming of the Lord Jesus as their Messiah. Biederwolf, in the introduction of his voluminous work titled *The Millennium Bible*, states that for 20 years he did not make one single reference in his preaching to the return of Christ. Later he was moved to minister on the subject. Knowing that his knowledge of eschatology was almost nil, he made a thorough study of not only the doctrine of the second coming of Christ but of all eschatological references throughout the Bible. The result of his research is his 728-page book.

Beware of Date Setting

Some people have become overzealous concerning the future and have gone beyond the Bible. A nationally known preacher said some years ago that the Holy Spirit had revealed to him that Christ would return during that decade, but the decade passed and Christ did not return. Henry H. Halley says he thinks some people will be disappointed if Christ does not adhere to the schedule they have made out for Him!

We know that Jesus is coming, not according to man's schedule but in God's own time. No one knows when that time will be. Jesus said that even He did not know the day or hour: "No one knows about that day or hour, not even the angels in heaven, nor the Son, but only the Father" (Mark 13:32).

Nonetheless, the Lord does reveal a great deal to us about His Son's return and the events to follow. Though He does not name the day nor the hour, "surely the Sovereign Lord does nothing without revealing his plan to his servants the prophets" (Amos 3:7). Just as "God spoke to our forefathers through the prophets at many times and in various ways" (Hebrews 1:1), He still speaks to us today through the writings of those prophets.

It is a fact that wild, speculative statements concerning prophetic scriptures have caused confusion. Just before World War II and during the early years of that global conflict, some well-meaning individuals tried to show that Benito Mussolini, and later Adolph Hitler, was the Antichrist. In fact, an entire book was written supporting the contention that Mussolini was Antichrist.

These and other such ill-founded speculations placed eschatology in a bad light during those days, and for years afterward a minister was thought to be neither scholarly nor tuned to the times if he preached on things to come. Those ministers who preached often concerning future events were referred to as prophecy preachers and were looked on as quaint or "not quite all there."

Lately there is definitely an accelerated interest in the future. Law, order, and morals are crumbling; and man is taking a new look into God's Word, where he is finding a description of these days and what lies ahead.

We find a clear-cut description of contemporary world society and an admonition for ourselves in 2 Timothy 3:1-5:

> There will be terrible times in the last days. People will be lovers of themselves, lovers of money, boastful, proud, abusive, disobedient to their parents, ungrateful, unholy, without love, unforgiving, slanderous, without self-control, brutal, not lovers of the good, treacherous, rash, conceited, lovers of pleasure rather than lovers of God—having a form of godliness but denying its power. Have nothing to do with them.

Test of Validity

Churchill commented, "You know I always avoid prophesying beforehand; it is much better policy to prophesy after the event has already taken place." A Greek proverb says that he who guesses best is the best prophet. Millennia ago Moses pondered this problem of a prophet's validity: "How can we know when a message has not been spoken by the Lord?" (Deuteronomy 18:21). He answers the question thus: "If what a prophet proclaims in the name of the Lord does not take place or come true, that is a message the Lord has not spoken. That prophet has spoken presumptuously. Do not be afraid of him" (v. 22).

What a practical test! Old Testament prophets who foretold the time, place, and manner of Christ's birth were bona fide prophets, because their predictions came true. Also, those stalwarts of God who foretold His coming again were true prophets. We know Christ died and was resurrected as He predicted. We also know that He is coming again!

But not all so-called prophets have been genuine. An example was William Miller, who led the great Millerite movement (1831-1845) with such zeal and conviction that he convinced thousands of people that Christ would return at a stated time, which, of course, did not happen. Such erroneous preaching appears as a rash on the otherwise clear complexion of eschatology. Prophecy is the ruddy glow of the good health of Christ's body, the church.

Hermeneutics—the science of interpretation and explanation—is of utmost importance in studying eschatology. Almost all Evangelical scholars give a literal interpretation to as much of the Bible as possible. David L. Cooper states in his work *When Gog's Armies Meet the Almighty in the Land of Israel*: "When the plain sense of Scripture makes common sense, seek no other sense; therefore, take every word at its primary, ordinary, usual, literal meaning unless the facts of the immediate context, studied in the light of related passages and axiomatic and fundamental truths, indicate clearly otherwise."

A prophecy may have a first and partial fulfillment hundreds of years before its full and complete fulfillment. An excellent example of this is Daniel's prediction in the ninth chapter of his book concerning the "abomination of desolation." This was partially fulfilled before Christ's birth by the desecration of the Jerusalem Temple by Antiochus Epiphanes, who actually offered a pig on the altar; but it will have its final fulfillment when the Antichrist commits an abominable act in the Jewish Temple during the Tribulation.

A little girl innocently asked, "If Jesus didn't mean what He said, why didn't He say what He meant?" We believe that Christ through the Holy Spirit did say what He meant, though for His own reasons He sometimes couched His statements in symbols and figures.

Purpose of Prophecy

The Bible is God's self-revelation; and it is man's only source of information concerning Jehovah's continuous, consistent account of His will, revealed through numerous prophets and writers to whom the character, inner thoughts, and purpose of the Almighty God is made clear. In His Word, He unfolds the great plan that was ever in His heart. A large part of His eternal plan has yet to see fruition, and that part of His plan we call prophecy.

In his work *Escape the Coming Night*, David Jeremiah writes of this last decade of the century and the approaching

GOD'S PROPHETIC WORD

end. Speaking of important lessons to be learned from prophecy, he says: "The New Testament tells us how prophecy can be a dynamic school. The Bible says that understanding the future will put our everyday problems into better perspective (Colossians 3:2). Prophecy provides us an urgency to reach others for Jesus Christ, to 'snatch others from the fire and save them' (Jude 23)."

Almost all prophecy relates to one of three general subjects: (1) the Gentiles, (2) the church, (3) the Jews. Prophecy of the Gentiles or Gentile nations is given in Daniel and Revelation, among other books. The church, the body of Christ, is often referred to in the New Testament, and numerous references predict that the church will be raptured or caught away to heaven. The Jews figure prominently in prophecy, and God is now returning the Jews to their ancient land in fulfillment of prophecy and preparatory to fulfillment of many other biblical prophecies about them.

End-Time Terms

Eschatology. The term is derived from a compound Greek word—*eschatos,* meaning last or latter, and *logos,* meaning discussion. Hence, eschatology is a discussion or study of last things or things to come. The word itself does not appear in the Bible.

Apocalypse. This is a name frequently given to Revelation, the last book of the Bible. It means disclosure or revelation.

Rapture. Though this word is not found in the Scriptures, its meaning so graphically depicts what will happen in the first phase of Christ's second coming that its use is widespread. Coming from the Latin word *rapio,* which means "to snatch away suddenly," the English word *rapture*, when used in reference to Christ's return, means "to carry away to sublime happiness." The New Testament Book of Titus refers to this event as "the blessed hope" (2:13), and so it is if we are daily serving the Lord.

The End. The Scriptures use this term often when discussing the end times. On several occasions Jesus used it. He said, "The harvest is the end of the age" (Matthew 13:39) and in verse 40, "So it will be at the end of the age." In Matthew 24, Christ also referred to the end times. "The end is still to come" (v. 6). "And then the end will come" (v. 14).

Last Days. This term, used repeatedly in the Scriptures, often refers to the end times. Two examples follow: "There will be terrible times in the last days" (2 Timothy 3:1). "You must understand that in the last days scoffers will come" (2 Peter 3:3).

CHAPTER 4

Money
and
Last Days

Money is a major subject of the Bible. Throughout His ministry, Christ often discussed finances, for He knew that money is a cornerstone of man's existence. Without an income we buy no clothes, groceries, utilities, or other necessary services. Money is so essential that the average American is threatened with economic disaster if he loses his income for only six weeks.

America has so grossly overspent that every American child is many thousands of dollars in debt at birth. Add to that the rising cost of housing, clothing, food, and education and the financial future of our children looks dismal.

A television panel discussing the national debt in October 1992 made some provocative statements. Comprised of a financial expert and two congressmen, the panel agreed that to pay off the national debt would require $47,000 from every wage earner in the United States.

END TIMES

The panel also pointed out that if a business begun at Christ's birth had lost $1 million a day until the present, it would still take 700 more years to lose $1 trillion. Yet our national debt is $4 trillion (1993) and at the present rate of increase will be $13 trillion by the year 2000. Americans love money so much that we are willing to spend our children into bankruptcy.

This is such a materialistic age that one does not have to practice witchcraft or be hoodwinked by some cult to be a worshiper at the altar of materialism. The fact is, most of us are vulnerable at the point of money. We like to own things. Some of us just like to buy for the thrill of buying. Christ warned, "Watch out! Be on your guard against all kinds of greed; a man's life does not consist in the abundance of his possessions" (Luke 12:15).

Not only does America overspend for possessions, but we also buy much more food than our body needs. Jesus said that at His return people would be eating and drinking—implying that much of mankind would be living in luxury. More than half the population of America and Europe is overweight, and Americans spend over $14 billion each year on diet formulas. Health authorities say Americans need to lose 1 billion pounds of fat!

Ours is a generation of mammon (money) worshipers. The battle cry is buy! buy! charge! charge! On an average day there are 43 million credit card charges. Many Americans charge whether or not they have money to pay. Therefore, bankruptcy has become so commonplace and acceptable that recently there were over one million bankruptcies in the U.S. courts at one time. People love money enough to cheat, lie, steal, overwork, or kill for it. That is why the apostle Paul wrote, "The love of money is a root of all kinds of evil. Some people, eager for money, have wandered from the faith and pierced themselves with many griefs" (1 Timothy 6:10).

Antichrist and Money

The New Testament has much to say about the end times and money. Revelation 13 discusses three subjects: (1) a world ruler, whom the Scriptures call *Antichrist*, (2) Satan worship as the universal state religion, (3) and money.

"He [the world ruler] also forced everyone, small and great, rich and poor, free and slave, to receive a mark on his right hand or on his forehead, so that no one could buy or sell unless he had the mark, which is the name of the beast or the number of his name" (vv. 16, 17). This reference, discussing the last half of the Tribulation period, foretells a last-day development that will require more than just possessing money in order to purchase goods. The world ruler will insist on being worshiped. He will receive power, authority, and his throne from Satan (v. 2). (Revelation 12:9 says that the dragon, mentioned in verse 2, is Satan.) Five times the chapter uses the term *worship*. So the rule of the Beast is more than the secular rule of a world dictator.

That world ruler will not be content to be sovereign throughout the earth. Having obtained his power, great authority, and throne from Satan, he will ultimately, like Satan, insist on being worshiped. He will tell the world to worship him or die (v. 15). It seems that receiving the mark of the Beast will include an agreement to worship the world ruler. In other words, if a person agrees to worship him and demonstrates that agreement by carrying a mark on his hand or forehead, he will be able to buy and sell. However, Revelation 14:11 solemnly warns, whoever takes the mark and worships the Beast will be doomed to hell.

Admonition of James

The apostle James also discussed money and the last days. A casual reading of chapter 5 would seem to indicate that the writing was directed to the unbelieving wealthy of James' day. However, in James 1:2 he addresses his readers as "my brothers." He was also writing to you and me in these end times. Verse 3 says, "You have hoarded wealth in the last days." God's Word does not forbid our having money. Some of the great leaders of the Bible, especially some in Old Testament times, were wealthy. On the other hand, the Bible repeatedly warns against allowing riches to possess us.

Paul the apostle wrote to the Corinthian church, admonishing them to hold their possessions loosely. He said, "The time is short. From now on . . . those who buy something [should act] as if it were not theirs to keep; those who use the things of the world, as if not engrossed in them. For this world in its present form is passing away" (1 Corinthians 7:29-31).

James wrote with the same urgency. Calling the times "the last days," he accused, "You have lived on the earth in pleasure and luxury" (v. 5, *NKJV*). All of us must be careful in this affluent time to be more concerned about God's will for our lives than about luxuries and pleasures. Supporting God's work must have preeminence over buying pleasure and luxury.

In verse 8 James took the long view concerning the basics of our commitment. Still emphasizing the end times, he said, "Be patient. Establish your hearts, for the coming of the Lord is at hand" (*NKJV*). One minute after Christ returns, our "treasure" (v. 3, *NKJV*) and our pleasures and luxury (v. 5) will have become as nothing. Then, only patient, established hearts will count. May God help us to keep money in proper perspective as we await the soon return of our Redeemer!

Christ on Finances

Jesus often referred to money. He instructed Peter to go fishing to find money to pay taxes, He discussed Caesar's portrait on a coin, He told of a servant who buried his master's money, and He overturned the money changers' tables in the Temple. Christ also referred to rich people who were destitute spiritually and to a poor widow who gave all she had in a Temple offering. He was keenly aware of the importance of money.

Our Lord dealt with finances a great deal in Matthew 6. He said not to "announce it with trumpets" (v. 2) when giving offerings but to be modest, even secretive, about giving. It is much better to lay up treasures in heaven than on earth, He taught, emphasizing that our hearts will be where our treasures are.

Jesus emphasized that we have to make a conscious decision about money. It must serve us—we must not serve it. Listen to His straightforward warning: "No one can serve two masters. Either he will hate the one and love the other, or he will be devoted to the one and despise the other. You cannot serve both God and Money" (Matthew 6:24). It seems that Christ was speaking of human masters and servants until He said, "You cannot serve both God and Money." He stressed that we will serve either one or the other.

As we reach the end of this age, we must not be distracted by the love of money and what it will buy. Our Lord taught that we are not to be overwrought even about life's necessities—not about food nor about clothing. He said, "Seek first [God's] kingdom and his righteousness, and all these things will be given to you as well" (Matthew 6:33).

It is obvious that Christ is driving the point home to us that money cannot be our god in our home, on the job, or in our aspirations. He insists that we maintain a proper attitude about it. He does not mind our having money, but money must not have us. If so, it becomes our god, for we cannot serve both Christ and money.

Jesus taught that it is better to give than receive, better to share than to keep. In fact, a most significant law of happiness and spiritual success was laid down by God in the Old Testament and by Christ in the New. First, look at what Jesus said: "Give, and it will be given to you. A good measure, pressed down, shaken together and running over, will be poured into your lap. For with the measure you use, it will be measured to you" (Luke 6:38).

Everything our Lord said was vital and of eternal significance. He gave this reference from Luke as an anchor, a rule—and if we will adhere to it, we will discover an important key to victorious living. James the apostle warned that some "have hoarded wealth in the last days." Giving and hoarding are totally opposite concepts, and Christ insisted that we share freely.

Jesus said that we must give. He did not say we should do so with the anticipation of receiving. But He did say that if we give we will receive back bountifully, though both what we give and what we receive in return may not always be in dollars and cents.

Keep an Open Hand

With Christ's law of giving and receiving in mind, what

should we do about giving to God? Remember, He promised that if we give, the return will be good measure, pressed down, shaken together, running over, and poured into our laps. What a great promise from a great Lord!

Are you openhanded toward God? This is no "give me a twenty and you will get back a hundred" doctrine. It is simply examining where we stand in light of Christ's law on giving. A threadbare yet great maxim says, "You can't outgive God." We need to reinstitute that philosophy in our lives in these end times. God's work needs the finances to reach a lost world, and we need to grow in Christ by complying with His admonition to give.

If we gave $1 in offerings 30 years ago, should we not give $5 now? If then we gave $1 in Sunday school, $1 in morning worship, and $1 in the evening, should we not give $15 on Sunday now? We give three to five times as much for everything we buy today. Why not apply that percentage of increase when giving to the Lord? Jesus lays down a great law about giving freely that can be overlooked at great loss.

While Christ stressed the importance of giving in the New Testament, God himself was just as emphatic in the Old Testament. Speaking through Moses concerning the poor Jews in their newfound homeland of Canaan, He said, "Give generously to him and do so without a grudging heart; then because of this the Lord your God will bless you in all your work and in everything you put your hand to" (Deuteronomy 15:10). There again is that same promise Christ made in the New Testament—give and it shall be returned to you, bountifully!

Robbers Always Lose

However, the polestar Old Testament reference on giving

(Malachi 3:8-10) has to do with our tithes and offerings. What God said about it over 2,500 years ago certainly applies to these last days also.

"Will a man rob God? Yet you rob me. But you ask, 'How do we rob you?' In tithes and offerings. You are under a curse—the whole nation of you—because you are robbing me. Bring the whole tithe into the storehouse, that there may be food in my house. Test me in this," says the Lord Almighty, "and see if I will not throw open the floodgates of heaven and pour out so much blessing that you will not have room enough for it."

What strict talk, but what rich promises! Note three things God stresses: (1) Robbing Him brings a curse; (2) He challenges us to "test" Him; (3) His return for our giving is great. Some argue that this Old Testament reference to tithing does not apply today—but I have never heard a tither propound that argument! The fact is, it is an Old Testament standard laid down by God and substantiated by Christ and the New Testament. The doctrine of tithing does apply to you and me today. The most important check written in my home each month is the tithing check to our local church.

However, the point here is not just whether tithing is biblical, but the emphasis also deals with the theme of giving, which runs like a gold cord throughout the Bible. Why debate tithing when God attaches such a great blessing to it? Why not accept God's standard for giving and then reap the incredible benefits promised? It seems to me that I would be foolish not to participate. Why lose—why be under a curse—when I can be so bountifully blessed by my heavenly Father? I am eager to tithe and give in offerings and then stand back and see how God will bless. He always keeps His word.

MONEY AND LAST DAYS

The plan in both Testaments is that I give, and give freely. Then God in turn gives to me freely. He promises that He will use the same measure to return blessings to me that I use to give to Him and others. What a great plan God has devised, and what a great decision the believer makes when he decides to accept and follow it in these end times. His plan for giving works.

CHAPTER 5

The RAPTURE

The taking of hostages by some Middle Eastern countries during recent times has been an awful blight on world society. One poor man held against his will for years was Robert Polhill, a 55-year-old professor at the Beirut University in Lebanon. He was captured and held hostage for 39 months. On April 22, 1990, he was released, after 1,183 days of captivity. The world media carried the joyful report of his being freed. Some of his first words were "It's a great pleasure to be free again."

Likewise, when our Lord comes and delivers His followers from the pain, suffering, and disappointment of this earth, we may well shout, "It's a great pleasure to be free!" That is what the Rapture will bring—freedom. Not only will we be freed from earth's ties, but we will be ushered into heaven with all of its joys, pleasures, and associations. That will be a great pleasure indeed!

The Rapture is not just the wistful thinking of weary

followers. It is a paramount doctrine of the Bible, for the hope of the return of Christ pervades the New Testament. The coming of the Lord is called the blessed hope (Titus 2:13), the purifying hope (1 John 3:2, 3), and the comforting hope (see 1 Thessalonians 4:18, KJV). Christ is coming again. Most of the world's population will miss the Rapture; nonetheless, millions will go from around the world.

It will be a time of worldwide consternation for those left. Driverless cars, interrupted surgeries, planes without pilots and empty lecterns will devastate parts of the world. Muslim, Hindu, and Buddhist countries will not be adversely affected, because of their lack of Christians in leadership; but countries like America will be. In his book *The Rise of Babylon*, Charles H. Dyer estimates that as many as 28 million Americans may go in the Rapture. Such a loss would so cripple our country that it would go into the Tribulation greatly weakened as a world power.

It is not only possible but even probable that the Rapture will take place soon. Out of the chaos that follows, Antichrist will arise with sensible and hopeful solutions, and he will become the world ruler partly through acceptance and partly by force. One great "comfort" of the Rapture, spoken of by the apostle Paul, is to escape the Tribulation, which will follow. Yes, Christ is coming again.

Christ Could Come Today

Many of us today eagerly anticipate the return of Christ—that epoch-making event, the Rapture, or the translation of the church—which could take place at any moment. His coming will be secret and unannounced, and we who are His followers will be whisked away to be forever with the Lord (1 Thessalonians 4:17).

THE RAPTURE

Though we may get excited about this truth, it must surely sound preposterous to people who hear it for the first time. Yet, that notable book the Bible, clearly and emphatically teaches the doctrine of the Rapture. "Listen, I tell you a mystery: We will not all sleep, but we will all be changed—in a flash, in the twinkling of an eye, at the last trumpet. For the trumpet will sound, the dead will be raised imperishable, and we will be changed" (1 Corinthians 15:51, 52).

There will be millions who will never die, and if you and I are living for Jesus when He returns, we will be among those millions. We will take a "plain-air trip" through the sky, past the moon, the stars, the sun, and into heaven. The Bible speaks of how quickly we will be changed—"in a flash, in the twinkling of an eye" (1 Corinthians 15:52).

We will be changed suddenly, as quickly as you blink your eye, and you do that in eleven one-hundredths of a second! Little wonder that Christ likened His coming to that of a thief, who slips in and quickly and quietly carts off valuables from a home. The Lord will return and secretly sweep us from this world. We will vanish into thin air—think of it! Those left will not even be aware of the event until it is all over.

Since my childhood I have known about the scriptural teaching of the return of Christ. The circumstances that forcefully brought that truth to my young mind are indelibly stamped upon my consciousness. I was with Mother in the backyard of our home, where she was sweeping leaves with a brush broom. Hearing a rumbling in the distance, she stopped sweeping, looked toward the east, the direction of the noise, where a thunderhead loomed. "Someday," she said in her saintly, quiet voice, "Christ is coming back. And

He will come in a cloud, perhaps like that one," she concluded, as she pointed toward the thunderhead.

The rumbling, the cloud, and the thought of Christ's appearing perturbed me. And all the while the noise in the cloud's direction became louder. Soon, however, my mind was set at ease, for I heard the faint, distant blowing of the whistle of a freight train, and I knew that the train accounted for the rumbling sound. Long since I have learned that the Lord did not give the doctrine of the Rapture to frighten little boys but to comfort and encourage believers.

The concept of being translated is hardly conceivable to us mortals, for the only way we have seen people depart from this life has been through death. However, a few people in biblical history, such as Enoch and Elijah, did not die.

Jesus and His Return

Our Lord often spoke of His second advent. Such statements as "When the Son of Man shall come in his glory," "The Son of Man shall come," or "I will come again" intersperse His teachings. The night before His ignominious death at Calvary, Christ spoke tenderly to His disciples about His return. He endeavored to prepare them for His leaving by telling them why He was going and that He would come back. His compassionate words were spoken to His tired disciples on that dark night of the Betrayal, and we look deep into His concerned heart as He endeavored to bolster the courage of His wavering disciples. He said: "Do not let your hearts be troubled. Trust in God; trust also in me. In my Father's house are many rooms; if it were not so, I would have told you. I am going there to prepare a place for you. And if I go and prepare a place for you, I will come back and take you to be with me that you also may be where I am" (John 14:1-3).

THE RAPTURE

Though His disciples did not comprehend the discussion that night, it must certainly have buoyed their faith the following months and years when they remembered His emphatic statement that He would come again and take them away. Surely they anticipated His return every day. Christ will keep His word and will come again for His disciples. They will be resurrected at the Rapture. "The dead in Christ will rise first," Paul wrote. Therefore, when Christ comes back, all of those saints who have died since the Cross will rise, and those living will be translated, and together we will all be taken by Christ to heaven. (See 1 Thessalonians 4:16, 17.)

The Lord's Supper

When you participate in that very sacred ordinance, the Communion, you are giving testimony to your faith in the return of Christ. At that first supper, the 12 disciples met with the Lord in the Upper Room for the evening meal. While the dining progressed, Judas pondered the betrayal, and Christ knew his thoughts. The other disciples were oblivious of the fact that their treasurer contemplated such a dastardly act.

The drama and suspense that transpired that evening could never be fully reenacted on the stage. Jesus' heart was heavy. Added to the gigantic burden of His imminent death was the heartbreak that one of His disciples would betray Him to His enemies and that the others, one by one, would forsake Him and flee. Nonetheless, against this backdrop Jesus confidently instituted the Lord's Supper.

This holy event became an ordinance of the church; and every time you and I take Communion, we are saying by our actions that Christ is coming back. The Bible declares it:

"The Lord Jesus, on the night he was betrayed, took bread, and when he had given thanks, he broke it and said, 'This is my body, which is for you; do this in remembrance of me.' In the same way, after supper he took the cup, saying, 'This cup is the new covenant in my blood; do this, whenever you drink it, in remembrance of me.' For whenever you eat this bread and drink this cup, you proclaim the Lord's death until he comes" (1 Corinthians 11:23-26).

Penning their thoughts under the inspiration of the Holy Spirit, the writers of the New Testament often referred to Christ's coming. Three hundred and nineteen verses are devoted to the subject. On an average one verse in every 25 is given to the theme, making it a major doctrine of the New Testament. Both 1 and 2 Thessalonians are generally believed to have been the first two Pauline books written, and both clearly set forth the doctrine of the return of Christ. In fact, 1 Thessalonians 4:16, 17 is the polestar reference concerning the translation of the church. All of the epistles anticipate the return of Christ, and the Book of Revelation speaks almost entirely of His return and the events following. Any serious student of the Bible must concede that the return of Jesus Christ is an emphatic theme of the New Testament.

Church Fathers Expected Jesus

Many of the church leaders since Paul referred to the return of Christ. In the first century Ignatius of Antioch stated, "Christ was received up to the Father and sits on his right hand, waiting till his enemies are put under his feet." Irenaeus, who lived in the second century, said of Christ's return, ". . . appearing from heaven in the Glory of the Father, to comprehend all things under one head."

THE RAPTURE

Through the centuries men have spoken of Christ's return. Though during the Dark Ages sight of "the blessed hope" was almost completely lost, later the doctrine was proclaimed again. It was said of Wycliffe that he regarded the Redeemer's appearing as the object of the hope and constant expectation of the church of God.

John Calvin commented, "The Scripture uniformly commands us to look forward with eager expectation to the coming of Christ." John Knox testified, "We know that He shall return, and that with expedition." Martin Luther said, "I ardently hope that admist these interval dissensions on earth, Jesus Christ will hasten the day of His coming." The great songs of Charles Wesley reverberate with the doctrine of the return of Christ. He wrote:

O may we all be found
Obedient to Thy Word,
Attentive to the trumpet's sound,
And looking for the Lord.

For centuries the church has recited the Apostles' Creed. Every time we recite it, we reaffirm our faith in Christ's return. It reads in part: "I believe in God the Father Almighty, Creator of heaven and earth, and in Jesus Christ His only Son our Lord. . . . He ascended into heaven and sitteth on the right hand of God the Father Almighty. From thence He shall come to judge the quick and the dead."

We Expect Him to Return

When we speak of the imminent return of Jesus, we mean that He could come at any time. Many Christians feel that the event is quite probably very soon indeed. On the other hand, we do not know when He will come. Timewise, 75 years with God is as almost nothing, while for us it is a life span. However, signs foretold in the Scriptures such as those of the Tribulation, Armageddon, and the second coming of Christ to earth, cast distinct shadows on these days. Therefore, He could come at any moment.

Whereas a few years ago one seldom heard a sermon on the return of Christ, now Evangelical preachers often refer to the Rapture, the Tribulation, Armageddon, and the Millennium. There is a great deal of emphasis today upon things to come, and I believe the accelerated interest is the Holy Spirit's way of making us ever mindful of the Lord's imminent appearance. Billy Graham has said, "There is a foreboding in the air. Something phenomenal is about to happen; and that phenomenal happening will be the return of Christ." A national magazine recently stated, "For many, there exists a firm conviction that Jesus' Second Coming is literally at hand."

World Consternation

Some people who may not necessarily accept the teachings of the Bible—in fact, who may not even be aware of the futuristic aspect of the Scriptures—are saying that something must happen, that a cataclysmic event of worldwide proportions is inevitable. Since the splitting of the atom, statesmen, scientists, politicians, and men from other walks of life have asked with increasing frequency, "Where are we headed? What can we do? When will the end occur?"

Churchill said, "Our problems are beyond us," and Jean-Paul Sartre commented, "There is no exit from the human dilemma." Evangelist Billy Graham, in his book *World Aflame*, wrote "Our world is filled with fear, hate, lust, greed, war and utter despair. Surely the Second Coming of Jesus Christ is the only hope of replacing these depressing features with trust, love, universal peace and prosperity. For it the world wittingly or inadvertently waits."

In this perplexing hour Christ could well return. At any moment the believers could be whisked from this sin-blighted world, for the Lord will come at a dark hour. Paul admonishes us, "And do this, understanding the present time. The hour has come for you to wake up from your slumber, because our salvation is nearer now than when we first believed. The night is nearly over; the day is almost here. So let us put aside the deeds of darkness and put on the armor of light" (Romans 13:11, 12).

When Will Jesus Come?

Though we believe the coming of the Lord is near, we do not know when He will come. He could well come today or tomorrow. Nonetheless, we do not have any biblical grounds to justify our setting a date, saying that Christ will return at a certain time. Foolish conjectures have been made in the past. For example, it has been projected that in God's own providence the measurements of the Great Pyramid in Egypt correspond with certain prophetic truths, and by studying these measurements one can ascertain the future. However, it seems unreasonable that God would use the tomb of a dead heathen king to reveal the return of His living Son.

Some people earnestly believed that Christ would return at a certain date during the last century. Many either sold their property or gave it away, donned white robes, and went to mountaintops to await the appearance of the Lord. Further, the founder of the Jehovah's Witnesses sect, Charles Taze Russell, said that Christ came in 1914 but that His coming was of a spiritual nature and none saw Him. God has

END TIMES

not seen fit to adjust to men's foolish statements or predictions. Jesus discussed this matter of our not knowing just when He would come back. He emphasized that neither the angels nor He himself knew the date. He said, "Therefore keep watch, because you do not know on what day your Lord will come" (Matthew 24:42).

Writing to the church at Thessalonica, the apostle Paul emphasized that Christ would come unexpectedly: "For you know very well that the day of the Lord will come like a thief in the night" (1 Thessalonians 5:2). So we do not know just when Christ will come, but we do know that He will come unannounced, and we believe that His coming is near.

Some time ago a woman in the state of Georgia dreamed that she died and went to heaven. Upon arrival, she found decorations being mounted, a massive platform being built, and everyone busily engaged in work. Finally, she got the attention of someone and asked why all the preparation and whether something unusual was about to happen. "Haven't you heard," came the reply, "we believe the Father is about to send the Son for His bride, and we are preparing for the celebration."

When He Returns

In his infinite wisdom the Holy Spirit did not reveal to us in the Scriptures *when* Christ would return. However, He was most explicit in telling us just *how* the Lord Jesus would return, spelling out the event step-by-step. That momentous occurrence is dramatically described by the writer Paul: "For the Lord himself will come down from heaven, with a loud command, with the voice of the archangel and with the trumpet call of God, and the dead in Christ will rise first. After that, we who are still alive and are left will be caught

THE RAPTURE

up with them in the clouds to meet the Lord in the air. And so we will be with the Lord forever. Therefore encourage each other with these words" (1 Thessalonians 4:16-18).

Note the six emphatic points made in this reference: (1) the Lord himself is coming back, (2) the dead in Christ will rise first, (3) the living will be caught up, (4) we will meet the Lord in the air, (5) we will be with Christ forever, and (6) we are to encourage each other with the message.

1. *The Lord himself is coming back.* In the past, some important biblical events have been carried out by archangels. It seems that Michael's duty may have been to watch over the children of Israel (Daniel 12:1), while Gabriel has conveyed important messages to people in general. However, when the Rapture takes place, though an archangel is active, he is not the central figure. The Lord himself is coming after us. The event is too important to entrust to even an archangel.

Jesus who was born of Mary, ministered in Palestine, died on Calvary, arose triumphantly, and ascended into the heavens—that same Jesus is coming again. The Lord himself, the Christ who forgave your sins and mine, the Christ to whom we have prayed since our conversion—He will descend from heaven.

2. *The dead in Christ will rise first.* All those who have died in the faith since Calvary will rise. Those dead outside of Christ will not rise until the Great White Throne Judgment after the Millennium (Revelation 20). My saintly mother, who was immobile for two years before dying, the result of a paralytic stroke, will arise with a sound body, with all signs of the paralyzed arm, foot, and tongue gone. She will be physically perfect. Dad, who was a vibrant witness for the Lord until his death, will be able to speak without stuttering, for that impediment will be gone. *The dead in*

Christ will rise first. Those who have died at sea, the thousands buried in the catacombs of Rome, and all the other dead in Christ will be raised to life.

3. *The living will be caught up.* After the dead are raised, the living will be changed "in a flash, in the twinkling of an eye" (1 Corinthians 15:52), without experiencing death. If you and I are living then, we will be changed instantly from mortals to immortals. Our bodies will be made like Christ's glorious body; they will be immortal, perfect, painless, spiritual, and eternal. The Scriptures describe our future bodies: "But our citizenship is in heaven. And we eagerly await a Savior from there, the Lord Jesus Christ, who, by the power that enables him to bring everything under his control, will transform our lowly bodies so that they will be like his glorious body" (Philippians 3:20, 21).

4. *We will meet the Lord in the air.* Paul said that we "will be caught up with them in the clouds to meet the Lord in the air" (1 Thessalonians 4:17). All of the true Christians—boys, girls, men, and women—will be caught up. The unbelievers will be left on earth, the unregenerate dead will be left in the grave, but the dedicated followers of Christ will be raptured together with the resurrected righteous into the clouds.

This means that we will be reunited with our loved ones and friends who died in the faith. What a joyous occasion! Little wonder that the scriptural references confirming the Rapture often reflect exuberance and happiness, while those about the second coming of Christ to the earth speak of judgment and sternness which Christ will exercise in destroying His enemies.

After we have met our loved ones in the clouds, we will meet the Lord in the air—the marvelous, compassionate

Savior who forgave our sins, the One we have accepted by faith and about whom we have witnessed. Imagine the excitement of seeing Him for the first time!

5. *We will be with Christ forever.* Our seeing the Lord will not be just a temporary experience, but we will be in His holy presence forever. We will dwell with Him, the essence of purity, holiness, and intelligence. We will appear before him as He sits on the Judgment Seat, and we shall accompany Him at the Marriage Supper. Then we will come with Him back to earth and reign with Him a thousand years. Then in the new heaven and new earth we shall forever be with the Lord.

What great dividends we will reap throughout eternity by accepting Him now and following His teaching during our short lifetime. Someday soon all of this life will be over. How eager we become at times to be with the Lord, where forever we will be in His presence. The psalmist must have had such a longing when he wrote: "And I—in righteousness I will see your face; when I awake, I will be satisfied with seeing your likeness" (Psalm 17:15).

6. *We are to encourage each other with the message.* It is a blessed privilege for us to encourage each other in the faith. When the burdens are heavy and the tempest is raging, the believer should be told that Jesus says, "I am coming soon. Hold on to what you have, so that no one will take your crown" (Revelation 3:11). When our way is involved and our vision is earthbound, we are admonished to keep our faith directed heavenward, for "he will appear a second time, not to bear sin, but to bring salvation to those who are waiting for him" (Hebrews 9:28). When critics say that Christ is not coming, we should not waver but remember this promise: "For in just a very little while, 'He who is coming will come and will not delay'" (Hebrews 10:37).

Unwavering faith in the return of Christ makes for sturdy, healthy Christians. I do not know one believer who faithfully anticipates Christ's return who is not a confident, productive disciple. The Book of Hebrews calls our hope in the future an anchor: "We have this hope as an anchor for the soul, firm and secure. It enters the inner sanctuary behind the curtain, where Jesus, who went before us, has entered on our behalf. He has become a high priest forever, in the order of Melchizedek" (Hebrews 6:19, 20).

How Should We Live?

God expects us to live holy lives. This fact is certainly evident in many of the references concerning Christ's return. Careless living and indifference toward the things of God are not the marks of one who is looking for that blessed hope. Christ is coming after people who are right with Him, those who worship Him and prayerfully follow His teachings. Note what the Scriptures say:

> When Christ, who is your life, appears, then you also will appear with him in glory. Put to death, therefore, whatever belongs to your earthly nature: sexual immorality, impurity, lust, evil desires and greed, which is idolatry (Colossians 3:4, 5).

> Dear friends, now we are children of God, and what we will be has not yet been made known. But we know that when he appears, we shall be like him, for we shall see him as he is. Everyone who has this hope in him purifies himself, just as he is pure (1 John 3:2, 3).

These references suggest that Christ is coming after people who are living careful, godly lives and who are pure in heart. In fact, a criterion for living with God eternally, whether we go to heaven by death or the Rapture, was stated by our Lord as one of the beatitudes: "Blessed are the pure in heart, for they shall see God" (Matthew 5:8).

Nonetheless, it will be the righteousness of God in us that will make us eligible for the Rapture. We can all be grateful that the requirements will not be based on our personal goodness. None of us can of ourselves be good enough to go when Jesus comes. However, prayerful, godly, righteous living, trusting in the finished work of Calvary, will render us eligible to go. Therefore, we will go in the Rapture as the result of our confessing our sins to Christ, accepting Him into our hearts, and carefully following Him day by day.

Three Greek Words

Three specific words were used in the New Testament in reference to the coming of Christ:

1. *Parousia.* It is used about 25 times in the New Testament and is the word employed most frequently to describe the return of our Lord. It carries the idea of personal presence, meaning that Christ will return in person. (See 1 Corinthians 15:23; 1 Thessalonians 2:19; James 5:7, 8; 1 John 2:28.)

2. *Epiphaneia.* This word means appearing out of darkness. Such will be the case when Christ, "the bright and Morning Star" (Revelation 22:16), appears in this dark world. It is used in referring to the Rapture in these passages: 1 Timothy 6:14; 2 Timothy 4:8.

3. *Apokalupsis.* This word means to reveal or unveil. Today Christ is hidden from view; we perceive He is with us by faith. When He returns, He will be revealed in person. The word is used in these passages when referring to the Rapture: 1 Corinthians 1:7; Colossians 3:4; 1 Peter 1:7, 13.

END TIMES

Different Beliefs

When a person states that he believes the Bible teaches the Rapture of the church, it does not necessarily follow that he agrees with everyone else as to the time in the future that the Lord will return. There are four different views concerning the Rapture:

1. *Pretribulation Rapture.* The Bible refers to the Tribulation as being the most dreadful days that ever existed. Matthew 24 records Christ's graphic description of that seven-year period. The pretribulationist cannot comprehend the church's going through God's wrath. Instead, he anticipates the return of Christ, who "rescues us from the coming wrath" (1 Thessalonians 1:10). Most Evangelical Christians expect Christ to return before the Tribulation, hence they are pretribulationists. (Reasons we believe in a pretribulation Rapture are given on next page.)

2. *Partial Rapture.* Quite a few dedicated, Bible-loving Christians hold this view. They are pre-Tribulationists, but believe that the Scriptures teach that only the zealous, the holiest of the holy, will be worthy of the Rapture.

3. *Midtribulation Rapture.* Holding that Christ will return after the first three and one-half years of the Tribulation, adherents to this view teach that the church is promised tribulation and is in need of it for purging; that the Rapture will then take place, removing the church from the world so that the latter and more dreadful half of the Tribulation may run its course.

4. *Post-tribulation Rapture.* This view holds that the church will remain on the earth throughout the Tribulation, at the end of which the church will be raptured to meet the Lord in the air—on His way from heaven to earth. The church will join Christ and return to the earth with Him.

The Pretribulation Rapture

Although, as previously stated, many committed Christians hold views other than that Christ will return before the Tribulation begins, to most of us the Scriptures are clear on the doctrine of a pretribulation return of our Lord. Following are references supporting the doctrine.

1. *Christ will rescue us.* Regularly, the Bible uses the term wrath in discussing the Tribulation. Note Paul's words in 1 Thessalonians: "You turned to God from idols to serve the living and true God, and to wait for his Son from heaven, whom he raised from the dead—Jesus, who rescues us from the wrath to come" (1:9, 10).

2. *We are promised deliverance.* "Since you have kept my command to endure patiently, I will also keep you from the hour of trial that is going to come upon the whole world" (Revelation 3:10).

3. *Our departure ushers in the Tribulation.* "For the secret power of lawlessness is already at work; but the one who now holds it back will continue to do so till he is taken out of the way" (2 Thessalonians 2:7). We believe the "he" is the Holy Spirit within us, for we are temples of the Holy Spirit. Apparently, after the Rapture the Holy Spirit will be active in the world in the same capacity that He was before the Day of Pentecost.

4. *We escape wrath.* "For God did not appoint us to suffer wrath but to receive salvation through our Lord Jesus Christ" (1 Thessalonians 5:9).

5. *Biblical examples.* Both Noah and Lot escaped, and wrath followed. Christ named them as examples when speaking of His return.

The Holy Spirit used the doctrine of the Rapture to lead me to Christ. He pierced my heart with this truth one wintry

Sunday afternoon while I was a teenager still living at home with my parents. We were sitting around the fireplace and, as was customary, Dad was talking of spiritual things. On that particular day his mind dwelt on the Rapture. He said, "You know, it is going to be bad to be good but not good enough to go." Dad was perceptive, and he may have sensed my spiritual need. On the other hand, he may not have been aware of my need of Christ, for I went to church, sang in the choir, and did not have many of the open habits common to the unconverted. I was a good boy, but I had never had a personal encounter with Christ. I was good, but not good enough; I had not been born again.

Upon retirement that night, sleep fled, and my youthful heart, convicted of its sins, beat out the stinging truth: "It is going to be bad to be good but not good enough to go." The following weekend, during a Communion service, I gave my heart to Christ.

> Jesus is truly coming soon;
> It may be morning, night or noon.
> I'd like to write this in the sky
> So that people far and nigh
> Could look and see with their own eye:
> "Jesus is coming soon."
>
> Excuses will not answer then
> For what you or I have been.
> Our record will be waiting there
> To show if the Rapture or Tribulation we'll share.
> Will you live in mansions beyond compare?
> Jesus is coming soon.

THE RAPTURE

Won't you now dedicate your life
And turn completely from sin and strife?
Look and see God's flag unfurled,
Turn from Satan and his twirl,
And join me in telling to the world
Jesus is coming soon.

—*Written by the author soon after his conversion*

The Judgment of Believers

Adoniram Judson, a 25-year-old native of Massachusetts, went to Burma with his new wife, Ann, as a missionary in 1813. An unusually productive minister, he translated the Bible into Burmese and wrote a Burmese-English dictionary. Before his death in 1850, he and those he trained had a following of 500,000 believers.

After having lived in Burma for many years, Judson suffered extreme persecution. He was falsely accused of being an enemy agent. He was strung up by his thumbs for hours, unable to touch the ground, and suffered excruciating pain throughout his body. When he was returned to his tiny, sweltering cell after times of torture, his loving Ann would slip to the jail at night and whisper, "Hang on, Adoniram; God will give us the victory." During weeks of inhuman treatment, his faithful wife would come every night with the words, "Hang on, Adoniram; God will give us the victory."

One night Ann did not come, nor did she return the next

or the next. Judson was filled with apprehension, yet nobody told him she was at the point of death. Several months later he was released from jail hardly able to walk after the beatings and other torture. Immediately he began to search for his dear Ann, returning to the home where they had lived. A ragged, dirty little girl was outside their home when he arrived, so filthy that Judson did not recognize her at first as his own. Then he picked up his little girl and stumbled into the house, searching for his Ann.

He found her on a cot, hollow as a skeleton and delirious. Bending over her, his hot tears dripped on her face as he cried, "Ann, Ann, O my darling Ann." She stirred, opened her eyes, and said, "Hang on, Adoniram; God will give us the victory." Then she died. That man of God lost his beloved wife, yet he clung to his faith and courage. He went on to start more churches and win more Muslim converts.

The Bible says that someday saints like Adoniram Judson will stand before the "Reward Seat," where Christ himself will recognize them for their faithful service. Likewise, we all will appear before the judgment seat of Christ, where we will be judged not for our sins but for our service to the Lord. That judgment will take place in heaven.

When we go in the Rapture with Christ, we will live in heaven for seven years, while the Tribulation takes place on earth. While there, we will appear before the judgment seat of Christ and attend the Marriage Supper of the Lamb, then come back to the earth with the Messiah when He returns to rule the world for a thousand years.

Our finite minds cannot comprehend the glories that await us in heaven. Surely that place will be much more than we can even imagine it to be. For one thing, we will have time to associate more with each other. Also, we will

THE JUDGMENT OF BELIEVERS

be in the presence of the Holy Trinity—the Father, the Son, and the Holy Spirit. We will freely bow down and worship. Our limited minds cannot comprehend the harmony nor the purity of our association there with the Holy Trinity, with each other, and with the holy angels. If we will live for the Lord during our earthly life, we will someday dwell in that indescribable place He has prepared for us.

A Look at Heaven

We Christians eagerly anticipate heaven. Adam Clarke, whose commentaries on the Bible are studied around the world, talking about the hereafter when he was 84 years old, said, "I have passed through the springtime of my life. I have withstood the heat of summer. I have culled the fruits of fall. I am even now enduring the rigors of its winter, but at no great distance I see the approach of a new eternal springtime. Hallelujah!" What more could a loving God do for us than to let us live for Him here and then with Him there for eternity. Only the mind of our Sovereign Lord could conceive such a loving and generous plan.

Life in heaven may not be altogether as we sometimes hear it described. It is doubtful that we will only sit and strum on a harp while shading our eyes from glistening streets of gold. We may have harps, and there will be streets of gold, but that is not all there is to heaven. Rather, heaven is a place of action. We will be busy praising, serving, visiting, and worshiping.

Someone said that the door to heaven may have a sign reading, "No admission except on business." Pointing up our activity there, Scripture says, "His servants will serve him" (Revelation 22:3).

Heaven is also a place of unimagined beauty. John, the

writer of Revelation, described it "as a bride beautifully dressed for her husband" (Revelation 21:2). Think of the sheer beauty of a meticulously dressed bride meeting the groom. Womanhood is never lovelier than at that time. The Holy Spirit uses that illustration to put us in the proper frame of mind to ponder the beauty of heaven.

A little girl was quiet for an unusually long period of time while strolling on a clear night with her father. Finally he asked what was on her mind. "I was just thinking," the child answered, "if heaven with its stars is so beautiful wrong side out, how wonderful it must be on the other side."

The Holy Scriptures point out that heaven will be our dwelling place immediately after the Rapture (John 14:1-4) and that the Antichrist will curse us during the Tribulation—"those who live in heaven" (Revelation 13:6). Numerous names are applied to our future home: "my Father's house" (John 14:2); "the city with foundations, whose architect and builder is God" (Hebrews 11:10); "Mount Zion" (Hebrews 12:22); and "the Holy City" (Revelation 21:10).

Apparently we, the redeemed since the Cross, will occupy the most intimate place with Jesus Christ (Revelation 3:21). When the Old Testament saints are resurrected, apparently at the end of the Tribulation when Christ returns to the earth (Daniel 12:1, 2; Hebrews 11:39, 40), they will enjoy the city of God during the Millennium and afterward. It seems that they will be next to us in importance at that time. Also, innumerable angels will be present in heaven (Hebrews 12:22) for the precise purpose of serving us (Hebrews 1:14).

Your Life in Review

Did you know that when you get to heaven after the

Rapture you will be judged by Christ himself? Our acts during our Christian life will be evaluated. Just as a popular television show of another time reviewed the life of an individual, recalling persons and events which the individual may have nearly forgotten, so will our Christian lives be reviewed by Christ. The difference in the heavenly "This Is Your Life" will be that every unpleasant aspect will be aired, as well as the praiseworthy ones, whether it was good or bad. Our conduct back on earth will be reviewed: "For we must all appear before the judgment seat of Christ, that each one may receive what is due him for the things done while in the body, whether good or bad" (2 Corinthians 5:10).

Stephen Alford wrote in *Prophecy and the Seventies* about that judgment: "The Judgment Seat of Christ is an intensely solemn and searching aspect of prophetic truth. On account of this, it is not popular either in public preaching or in private discussion."

You see, this will not be a judgment of your sins but of your service. If Christ, the righteous Judge, finds you worthy, He will present rewards for faithful works. Paul referred to this judgment in his letter to the Romans: "You, then, why do you judge your brother? Or why do you look down on your brother? For we will all stand before God's judgment seat. It is written: '"As surely as I live," says the Lord, "every knee will bow before me; every tongue will confess to God."' So then, each of us will give an account of himself to God" (14:10-12).

The Bema of Christ

In New Testament times the *bema*, or reward seat, rested on a raised platform in the arena where sports events were held. The president or umpire sat on the bema where he watched the games and from which he presented rewards to the winning athletes. The bema was never used as a judicial bench but only as a reward seat.

Likewise, the judgment seat, or bema, of Christ will not be for the purpose of judging our sins but to reward us for our service. The songs you sang for His glory, the Sunday school class you taught, the sick you visited—if you did these things for Christ's praise and not for ulterior motives, they will bring rewards. What a soul-searching time it will be at the Bema!

The judgment seat of Christ will not convene to ascertain whether we will go to heaven, for we will already be there. Nor will it be to determine whether we will be removed and cast into hell. No, this will be a judgment of our Christian living, not for wrongs committed. We have already been forgiven for our sins, and we do not have to face judgment for them.

Our Three Judgments

While those who die outside of Christ will not be judged until after the Millennium, when they will be resurrected and judged at the Great White Throne (Revelation 20:11-15), we will not be judged at that judgment. Nonetheless, we do face judgments.

1. *Judged as sinners, a past judgment.* Before we accepted Christ we were already judged as sinners. Jesus himself said, "Whoever does not believe stands condemned already" (John 3:18). Being apart from God, we were under His wrath; we were judged. But then we repented of our sins and accepted Christ's atoning work for us, and we became His followers. Paul wrote, "Therefore, there is now no condemnation [judgment] for those who are in Christ

Jesus" (Romans 8:1), while the psalmist said, "As far as the east is from the west, so far has he removed our transgressions from us" (Psalm 103:12). Our sins are forgotten. We will not be judged for them.

2. *Judged as sons, a present judgment.* The heavenly Father through the Holy Spirit constantly judges us, reminding us, "This is the way; walk in it" (Isaiah 30:21). The Bible declares, "My son, do not make light of the Lord's discipline, and do not lose heart when he rebukes you, because the Lord disciplines those he loves, and he punishes everyone he accepts as a son" (Hebrews 12:5, 6).

3. *Judged as servants, a future judgment.* This judgment is yet to come, and it will take place at the judgment seat of Christ.

Christ Reviews

The omniscient Christ will be the judge at the Bema, for only Deity would be at all capable of carrying out the judging of the multiplied millions of people who will stand before the Judgment Seat. The Bible teaches that He will "bring to light what is hidden in darkness and will expose the motives of men's hearts. At that time each will receive his praise from God" (1 Corinthians 4:5).

The Sovereign Lord will bring to surface our hidden motives, whether good or bad, and He will show the inner thoughts of our hearts. This will be a completely impartial and just decision. Sometimes we are misunderstood and misjudged by people, but Christ will not misjudge.

Have you wondered just how this judgment will take place? The Scriptures are quite explicit in telling us:

> For no one can lay any foundation other than the one already laid, which is Jesus Christ. If any man builds

on this foundation using gold, silver, costly stones, wood, hay or straw, his work will be shown for what it is, because the Day will bring it to light. It will be revealed with fire, and the fire will test the quality of each man's work. If what he has built survives, he will receive his reward. If it is burned up, he will suffer loss; he himself will be saved, but only as one escaping through the flames (1 Corinthians 3:11-15).

It is generally taught that gold, silver, and precious stones denote service done for God's glory. On the other hand, wood, hay, and straw, though also representing work done, probably will be service rendered without giving the Lord the praise due Him. Things done in His vineyard yet performed for our own aggrandizement will be in the wood, hay, and straw category and will be burned up. The fire on that day must mean the searching judgment of God, "for our God is a consuming fire" (Hebrews 12:29).

Note that 1 Corinthians 3:15 reads, "If it is burned up, he will suffer loss; he himself will be saved, but only as one escaping through the flames." This verse implies that it may be possible to stay busy in God's work and yet lose our reward for that service at the Judgment Seat. May God help us not to witness, sing, pray, or preach just to draw attention to ourselves or to promote ourselves; but rather may we work to bring praise to Christ, for He alone is worthy of all praise and glory.

Our Works Burned

We hear a good deal about our rewards in heaven but very little about our losses. We seldom hear a sermon about the losses at the Bema. This is not a pleasant part of the Bible, but it too is God's inspired Word to us—a part that bears solemn warning. Our works can be consumed by fire from a holy Lord. We can suffer loss. In fact, we can find

THE JUDGMENT OF BELIEVERS

ourselves barely escaping the wrath of God. The unproductive believer will be sorely embarrassed; He will suffer shame. John promised that we will have no tears in heaven, but that is after the Millennium. At the Bema we may weep over squandered opportunities to give, to help, and to serve—opportunities which we forfeited.

In *God's Plan of the Ages*, Louis T. Talbot wrote, "All the unknown and unsung words and deeds of mercy; all the silent praises and prayers; all the selfish motives and idle words and bitter thoughts—these will go on parade before the all-seeing eye of the Son of God. What a solemn thought this is!"

The Lord places requirements on us according to our ability. It has been said, "God never looks at the amount on the face of the check, but at the balance on the stub." The Bible is clear on the point that if we are to be rewarded at the judgment seat of Christ, we must render dedicated, Christ-honoring service during this life.

The Five Crowns

God's Word refers to our rewards at the Bema as crowns. Apparently this means rewards such as the victory wreaths and crowns given in games during New Testament times (1 Corinthians 9:25; 2 Timothy 2:5). The crowns awarded at the Bema will not be of the kingly sort, for the king's crown is reserved only for Christ the King of kings. Our rewards will be victor's crowns, such as those the elders cast at the feet of Christ in worship and adoration (Revelation 4:10). The rewards we are to receive are categorized in five general areas.

1. *The incorruptible crown.* Mentioned in 1 Corinthians 9:25, this reward is bestowed for attaining mastery over the

"old man," and it awaits each of us who lives for the Lord with singleness of purpose. We are to live daily with the goal in mind.

2. *The crown of rejoicing.* This is a special reward for soulwinners. First Thessalonians 2:19, 20 affirms that souls won for our Master will make us worthy of this crown. What an award must await the apostle Paul, not only because of the Thessalonians he won to the Lord but for the host of others he led to Calvary as well. Daniel, of the Old Testament, wrote, "Those who are wise will shine like the brightness of the heavens, and those who lead many to righteousness, like the stars for ever and ever" (Daniel 12:3).

The Spirit may have had the crown of rejoicing in mind when He moved the apostle John to write, "I am coming soon. Hold on to what you have, so that no one will take your crown" (Revelation 3:11).

Louis T. Talbot told of a man who stood on a street corner years ago handing out Christian literature. Another man going home from work took one of the Christian tracts, read it, was convicted of his sins, and gave his heart to Christ. The new convert went back to the street corner to thank his benefactor for giving him the tract, but the man was not there. After several trips the new convert concluded that the Christian worker was either ill or had moved, so he secured tracts and began to regularly hand them out on the same street corner.

Later in a prayer meeting he related the account of his conversion and subsequent ministry with the tracts, and his unknown benefactor was in the congregation. The benefactor stood and said, "My friend, I became discouraged and gave up the tract ministry as useless—and now you have taken my crown." May the Lord help us to serve patiently and faithfully in the area where He has placed us.

3. *The crown of life.* When Satan storms the walls of our souls, threatening to break through, we must stand firm, trusting in the strength of Christ, remembering that "blessed is the man who perseveres under trial, because when he has stood the test, he will receive the crown of life that God has promised to those who love him" (James 1:12).

4. *The crown of righteousness.* Paul wrote to Timothy, "Now there is in store for me the crown of righteousness, which the Lord, the righteous Judge, will award to me on that day—and not only to me, but also to all who have longed for his appearing" (2 Timothy 4:8).

The saintly Paul, just before his decapitation, anticipated the crown of righteousness. Nonetheless, he will not receive it until "that day," that is, until he stands before the judgment seat of Christ.

5. *The crown of glory.* This seems to be a special reward for the faithful pastor who willingly feeds his flock week after week. The apostle Peter discussed the reward as follows: "Be shepherds of God's flock that is under your care, serving as overseers—not because you must, but because you are willing, as God wants you to be; not greedy for money, but eager to serve, not lording it over those entrusted to you, but being examples to the flock. And when the Chief Shepherd appears, you will receive the crown of glory that will never fade away" (1 Peter 5:2-4).

This never-fading crown is promised as a reward for unselfish, exemplary pastoral ministry. Many faithful men and women of God will receive this crown. Dedicated pastors who spend hours in prayer about sermons, about burdens of their members, and about spiritual needs of their congregation will be candidates for this reward. It is understandable that God has a special honor for the pastors who marry the young, bury the dead, comfort the brokenhearted, and lead sinners to the Lord Jesus. These unsung heroes who have cared for God's flock entrusted to them will be honored by Christ at the Judgment Seat.

Before leaving our discussion of the judgment seat of Christ, we should take a look at the Scripture's warning to us not to judge our brother but to leave judgment to Christ to be carried out at the Bema.

Beware of Judging Others

The Lord knows how human it is for us to criticize our fellow Christians. It is so easy for me to clearly see "the speck of sawdust" in your eye, while completely ignoring "the plank" in my own (see Matthew 7:3-5). Understandably, Christ called such biased attitudes sheer hypocrisy.

Our Lord taught, "Moreover, the Father judges no one, but has entrusted all judgment to the Son" (John 5:22). And Paul asked, "You, then, why do you judge your brother? Or why do you look down on your brother? For we will all stand before God's judgment seat" (Romans 14:10). Paul also wrote, "My conscience is clear, but that does not make me innocent. It is the Lord who judges me. Therefore judge nothing before the appointed time; wait till the Lord comes. He will bring to light what is hidden in darkness and will expose the motives of men's hearts. At that time each will receive his praise from God" (1 Corinthians 4:4, 5).

Romans 14:1-13 discusses the problem of Christians' judging one another. The believers Paul was addressing were concerned about eating certain things and observing certain days. Paul admonished them to receive the one weak in the faith (v. 1), because "God has accepted him"

(v. 3). He reminded them that they were not their brother's lord (v. 4). Then Paul admonished them not to judge a brother, "for we will all stand before God's judgment seat" (v. 10).

The story is told of a woman who looked from her kitchen window one morning at her neighbor's white clothes hanging on the line. She remarked, "Just look at the dingy spots on her sheets. Why doesn't she bleach them?" "The spots," a friend countered, "are not on your neighbor's sheets; they are on your windowpanes!"

Likewise, we are prone to be the most critical when we have the most unconfessed faults. Instead of sitting in judgment against each other, may we encourage and strengthen the brother who appears to be weak; then at the Judgment, Christ will not have to judge us for judging a fellow believer.

The Wedding Banquet

After we are judged and rewarded by our Lord, and before returning to the earth with Christ, we will attend the Marriage Supper of the Lamb. The Bible calls the church the bride of Christ, and the Marriage Supper will be a festive event celebrating the union of the Bridegroom with His bride. "Let us rejoice and be glad and give him glory! For the wedding of the Lamb has come, and his bride has made herself ready. Fine linen, bright and clean, was given her to wear" (Revelation 19:7, 8).

The joyous event will take place between the Rapture and the second coming of Christ to the earth. Apparently, the Marriage Supper follows the Bema, for the Bible says: "Fine linen, bright and clean, was given her to wear" (Revelation 19:8). Fine linen stands for the righteous acts of the saints. This implies that the church has already been accepted and rewarded at the Judgment.

This banquet will take place in heaven. No other location could qualify for such an occasion. The judgment seat of Christ is in heaven; and after the Marriage Supper, Christ will return to earth, so the event has to transpire in glory.

> And in that holy company,
> May you and I find place,
> Through worth of Him who died for us,
> And through His glorious grace;
> With cherubim and seraphim,
> And hosts of ransomed men,
> To sing our praises to the Lamb,
> And add our glad amen.
>
> —Author Unknown

CHAPTER 7

The WORLD AFTER the RAPTURE

We can easily imagine all kinds of reports and explanations being given concerning the multiplied millions of missing persons after the Rapture. A few examples might read as follows:

"Our weekly Optimist Club luncheon was in session and Joe was giving a report on our assistance to the Boys Club when between words he was gone—just like that!—vanished while we were looking at him!"

"I had come home from the office for lunch. My husband had picked up the baby at the nursery, and we were eating together. Before returning to work I stepped into the bedroom for a moment, and when I came out Jim and the baby were gone. Jim never just walked out like that. I don't understand it. They couldn't evaporate into thin air—could they?"

"All the news this evening will be given to the so-called

Great Disappearance that took place at noon today. Our regular programming for the entire evening has been cancelled so that we may keep you informed as news comes in about this most unusual worldwide event."

Analysts and philosophers will give their explanation of the mass disappearance, while people throughout the world will search for their missing friends and loved ones. However, like Enoch, they will not be found, for Christ will have taken them to heaven so that they might escape the horrendous times that will follow here on earth.

The Tribulation

After the church is taken out of the world, evil will increase on the earth. Besides, God will pour judgments on the world. Christ referred to those days as a time of great distress; and in the Olivet Discourse (Matthew 24), He talked at length about that terrible time. In fact, the most trying days that ever existed will occur during the seven-year period, and there will never be times like them again.

We thought that Hitler's Auschwitz or Japan's prison camps during World War II were unspeakably merciless, but Jesus said the Tribulation will be worse: "For then there will be great distress, unequaled from the beginning of the world until now—and never to be equaled again. If those days had not been cut short, no one would survive, but for the sake of the elect those days will be shortened" (Matthew 24:21, 22).

During that fearful period millions of people will die (Revelation 6:8; 9:15), and others will desire to die, but death will flee (Revelation 9:6). The Tribulation is so important that most of Revelation (chapters 6-19) is given to a thorough discussion of it; further, part of the Book of Daniel

THE WORLD AFTER THE RAPTURE

describes it, while numerous references are made to the period in many other places in the Bible. (See Jeremiah 30:7; Ezekiel 38:16; Malachi 4:5.)

Not only does the last book of the Bible discuss the apostate religious system, the Antichrist, and the False Prophet, but it also graphically details the judgments of God upon a Christ-rejecting world. It describes those judgments as seals (Revelation 6), trumpets (8:2—9:21; 11:15), and bowls or vials (16:1-21). God's other judgments are upon the apostate church (ch. 17) and upon the Beast (ch. 19).

The first of these judgments, the seals, could start happening soon, that is, immediately after the Rapture. In his book *When Dust Shall Sing*, George Britt wrote, "Many discerning Bible students today can see the storm clouds of the Tribulation already gathering and casting their shadows upon this troubled, perplexed world." Some of the seal judgments will take place immediately after the Rapture.

The Prophet Daniel

Since early childhood you have heard of Daniel in the den of lions. God's locking their jaws and bringing Daniel out unscathed makes for a stirring and graphic story from God's Word. The account is found in Daniel 6. The whole episode came about because Daniel was a man of prayer. He refused to pass up his prayer time, even though he knew that the act of praying would lead him from the king's palace to the lion's den; he valued prayer higher than life. Though most of us know about the lion's den of chapter 6, fewer of us know about the Seventy Weeks of chapter 9. However, that history-making experience came about also because Daniel was a man of prayer. Note that in the first few verses of the chapter the prophet was reading in the

Book of Jeremiah, and then he sought God in prayer and fasting: "In the first years of his reign, I, Daniel, understood from the Scriptures, according to the word of the Lord given to Jeremiah the prophet, that the desolation of Jerusalem would last seventy years. So I turned to the Lord God and pleaded with him in prayer and petition, in fasting, and in sackcloth and ashes. I prayed to the Lord my God and confessed" (Daniel 9:2-4).

Read Daniel's prayer in Chapter 9; hear him as he confesses his sins and those of his people; feel his heartthrob as he implores God in verse 19: "O Lord, listen! O Lord, forgive! O Lord, hear and act! For your sake, O my God, do not delay, because your city and your people bear your Name."

It was after reading God's Word that Daniel was moved to pray the great prayer of chapter 9. Also, it was after this time of Bible reading and prayer that he was morally and spiritually prepared to receive the revelation of the incredible prophecy known as the Seventy Weeks.

This grand old prophet—Berkeley says he was at least 84 years old—had learned the combination that unlocks the door to spiritual opportunities; that is, he had learned to study the Bible, to fast, and to pray. Though he lived 2,500 years ago, he had come upon this ever-current formula that led him to spiritual heights with God. That same time-tested formula will work today for you and me.

Prayer will bring results for us as surely as it did for Daniel. Jesus promised, "When you pray, go into your room, close the door and pray to your Father, who is unseen. Then your Father, who sees what is done in secret, will reward you" (Matthew 6:6).

Thirty minutes in prayer each day will revolutionize any

Christian's life. Prayer brings us to the basics of our spiritual existence, as it did Daniel. No other activity will remove the froth and chaff of everyday life and let us see clearly with a spiritual eye. It may take 20 minutes of the 30-minute prayer time to "close the door," but once our mind closes out distractions, the 10 minutes of holy communion is worth the battle. Daniel knew that.

What Gabriel Said

In just four verses of chapter 9, the angel gave Daniel a panoramic view of things to come from Daniel's day until the Cross, plus seven years that is still to take place in the future. The message brought by Gabriel to Daniel is as follows:

> "Seventy 'sevens' are decreed for your people and your holy city to finish transgression, to put an end to sin, to atone for wickedness, to bring in everlasting righteousness, to seal up vision and prophecy and to anoint the most holy. Know and understand this: From the issuing of the decree to restore and rebuild Jerusalem until the Anointed One, the ruler, comes, there will be seven 'sevens,' and sixty-two 'sevens.' It will be rebuilt with streets and a trench, but in times of trouble. After the sixty-two 'sevens,' the Anointed One will be cut off and will have nothing. The people of the ruler who will come will destroy the city and the sanctuary. The end will come like a flood: War will continue until the end, and desolations have been decreed. He will confirm a covenant with many for one 'seven.' In the middle of the 'seven' he will put an end to sacrifice and offering. And on a wing of the temple he will set up an abomination that causes desolation, until the end that is decreed is poured out on him" (Daniel 9:24-27).

What does the use of the term "sevens" in this passage

mean? In the case of Daniel's Seventy Weeks, a seven is equal to seven years, with each day standing for a year.

The concept of a "week" or "seven" meaning seven years was not new to the people of Israel. When Jacob had worked seven years for Rachel and was given Leah instead, Laban told Jacob, "'Finish out this daughter's bridal week; then we will give you the younger one also, in return for another seven years of work.' And Jacob did so. He finished out the week with Leah, and then Laban gave him his daughter Rachel to be his wife" (Genesis 29:27, 28). This account along with other Old Testament passages gives testimony to the fact that the Jews recognized they could have a week of days or a week of years.

Four Hundred and Ninety Years

Gabriel foretold a span of time 490 years in length, divided as follows: (1) 7 weeks, or 49 years; (2) 62 weeks, or 434 years; and (3) 1 week, or 7 years.

1. *The 49 years.* Daniel's Seventy Weeks are primarily directed to the Jews. The prophecy speaks of *your people, your holy city, the most holy, the Anointed One, covenant, sacrifice, and offering.* These are Jewish terms directed to the Jewish people. Nonetheless, the prophecy, especially the Seventieth Week, ultimately has to do with all mankind. The reference to "seven 'sevens'" (49 years) in verse 25 is significant, because from the time permission was given Zerubbabul to rebuild the city of Jerusalem until it was finished was 49 years (445-396 B.C.).

2. *The 434 years.* These years date from the completion of the rebuilding of Jerusalem until Christ died at Calvary. Again, the numbers in the prophecy were precise: there were exactly 434 years of 360 days each between these events, just as Gabriel predicted. Chronologists such as Sir

Robert Anderson testify to the dating of the Seventy Weeks. How amazingly accurate is God's Word!

3. *The seven years.* This period will be discussed later. Remember that this is the only part of Daniel's prophecy which has not been fulfilled. Since the 69 "weeks" were fulfilled to the letter, we have little difficulty believing that God will see to it that this last week will also take place. This will be "a time of trouble for Jacob" (Jeremiah 30:7), "distress" (Matthew 24:29), and that horrid period discussed in most of Revelation (chapters 6-19).

Church Age Not Covered

Daniel's 69th week ended when our Lord died at Calvary—when He was "cut off" (Daniel 9:26). At that time the Jewish clock stopped; it has not sounded a tick since Jesus said, "It is finished" (John 19:30) and dropped His holy head and died. We are now living in a time which Old Testament prophets did not mention or see (Ephesians 3). We call this parenthetical time the church age—a time when, though the individual Jew may come to Christ if he desires, the age of grace turned from the Jewish nation to the Gentiles.

This gap between Daniel's 69th and 70th weeks is an indefinite period of time and will end when the Rapture takes place. Then Daniel's Seventieth Week will start, and will continue for a "week," or seven years. After the Rapture it will be as though God reaches down and starts the pendulum of the ancient Jewish clock, which will measure that last week.

The Final Week

Daniel's Seventieth Week (Daniel 9:27) is the same period

END TIMES

discussed in Christ's Olivet Discourse (Matthew 24) and John's seals, trumpets, vials, and other events (Revelation 6—19). With remarkably few words, Daniel gives us a panoramic view of that time which we call the Tribulation. First, he tells why it will take place—"to finish transgression" (9:24). Though the Jewish nation rejected Christ at Calvary, they will complete their transgression during the Tribulation.

When Christ returns to the earth at the close of the Tribulation, He will "put an end to sin" (v. 24), for the Jews will accept His atoning work done at Calvary. Then He will "bring in everlasting righteousness" (v. 24), meaning His thousand-year millennial reign. At that time Daniel's prophecy will be finished, and the "most holy" will be anointed. This anointing refers either to an anointing of Christ or to the anointing of the Holy of Holies in the Temple in the Millennium. The majority of Evangelical opinion leans toward the latter interpretation.

Verse 26 refers to the fall of Jerusalem in A.D. 70. However, the term *ruler* of that verse looks forward hundreds of years to a world ruler during the Tribulation, whom the Bible calls the Antichrist. The phrase reads, "the people of the ruler." It is believed that the Antichrist will come from the revived Roman Empire, and his people referred to here were the Romans who destroyed Jerusalem. It is significant that "war will continue to the end" (v. 26). Surely no one doubts the constant fulfillment of this clause.

If you have ever wondered just what kind of person the coming world ruler will be, then you should carefully study Daniel 9:27. Though we will look at this man later in detail, note that the verse says he will (1) make a seven-year treaty with the people; (2) after half that time, break his pledge and stop the Jews from all their sacrifices and offerings; and then (3) utterly defile the sanctuary of God.

His committing this abomination of desolation will signal the start of the latter half of the Tribulation, which Christ described as the most hideous time ever to exist (Matthew 24:21, 22).

People who live for God are the deterrent to the coming of this world ruler. When we, the body of Christ, are taken from the world, then this person, energized by Satan himself, will come to world leadership. Paul discussed this dictator at length in 2 Thessalonians 2:3, 4, 7:

> Don't let anyone deceive you in any way, for that day will not come until the rebellion occurs and the man of lawlessness is revealed, the man doomed to destruction. He opposes and exalts himself over everything that is called God or is worshiped, and even sets himself up in God's temple, proclaiming himself to be God. . . . For the secret power of lawlessness is already at work; but the one who now holds it back will continue to do so till he is taken out of the way.

The one who is holding him back (v. 7) apparently refers to the Holy Spirit, who dwells in us, God's children, for "your body is a temple of the Holy Spirit, who is in you" (1 Corinthians 6:19). We are the salt of the earth Jesus referred to in the Sermon on the Mount; and when we are moved out of the way, churlish imps of Satan will break loose upon the earth with their macabre works of destruction. The forces of hell will be headed up by the Antichrist, a mortal man right here on earth. It is believed he will be a European, emerging from the old Roman Empire (Daniel 7:8).

The European Economic Community

On Thursday night, October 28, 1971, the British

Parliament cast its historic majority vote favoring entrance into the European Common Market, effective January 1973. Concerning that momentous event the *Mobile* (Alabama) *Press* carried a report the next day, which read: "The British decision to join the Common Market brought Western Europe to the threshold of its strongest union since the nations involved were tied together as part of the Roman Empire 15 centuries ago. This time they were moving together by choice . . . building a free trade group that would rival the economic power of the United States."

The organization and development of the Common Market (also called the European Economic Community) may be the link between today's events and the Tribulation, for the Market may prove to be the actual revival of the old Roman Empire. From your world history studies you may remember that the Roman Empire was never defeated, but simply crumbled. The Bible seems to imply that that empire will extend into the Tribulation period, and many Bible students believe that it will be revived as a 10-nation federation.

This is where the European Economic Community (EEC) enters the picture. An article carried in *Time* magazine a few years after the beginning of the Market said, "The Common Market could someday expand into a ten-nation economic entity." Note the regular use of the term *10-nation* in those formative years—the same term the Bible uses. The immediate intent of the Market is to unite Europe economically, but quite likely the continent will ultimately unite militarily and politically also.

Jean Monnet, the originator of the Market in 1958, stated, "As long as Europe remains divided, it is no match for the [superpowers]. Europe must unite." Though some years ago we could not have imagined a "united states" of

Europe, today it is a reality. This fact could well be signaling the immediacy of the return of Christ and the closeness of the Tribulation.

The Great Statue

The prophet Daniel was caught up in a bizarre situation. Nebuchadnezzar had a most unusual dream but forgot what it was about, then demanded that Daniel and some others either recall and interpret his dream or die (Daniel 2). Typically, Daniel sought God about it, and at night Jehovah revealed both the dream and the interpretation.

Daniel was shown that the king had seen a statue representing four world empires, and chapters 7 and 8 tell Daniel's correlating visions. The statue, or image, had a head of gold, representing the Babylonian Empire (likewise, the lion of chapter 7 represented that empire). The breast and arms of silver (and the leopard of chapter 7 and the ram of chapter 8) foretold the Medo-Persian Empire. The belly and thighs of brass (and the leopard of chapter 7 and the goats of chapter 8) described the coming Grecian empire, while the legs of iron and 10 toes of iron and clay (and the beast with 10 horns of chapter 7; see also Revelation 17:12) represented the Roman Empire with its resultant 10 nations. The stone that was cut out of the mountain (see Daniel 2:45; also Revelation 11:15) is Christ himself who will break to pieces the 10 nations when He comes back to the earth following the Tribulation.

In studying this statue, you will note that it could not possibly stand forever, for it progressively weakens from head to toe, and its feet, being iron mingled with clay, give it a weak foundation, a foundation that Christ will crush with His kingdom that will last forever. This remarkable image is another of Daniel's incredible prophecies which, like his Seventy Weeks, foretells events right up to the time that Christ will return to earth to rule.

The Roman Empire

The Roman Empire was vast, and for hundreds of years it wielded complete rule over much of the world. The Scriptures appear to indicate that when it is revived, it will expand even further (Revelation 13:7). Only the feet and toes portion of the image lacks fulfillment. These 10 kingdoms do not have to fulfill only the area of the old Roman Empire but may reach even further.

Earlier it was noted that the emergence of the European Economic Community (EEC) may well be the beginning of the 10-nation federation represented by the 10 toes of Daniel's prophecy. We know that a 10-nation bloc will be in existence when Christ returns to the earth, which He will crush. The EEC certainly has the appearance of the rise of the biblically predicted 10-nation confederacy, and those nations comprising it are in the same general area as the old Roman Empire. At this writing EEC has 12 members; but if it is indeed the fulfillment of Daniel's prediction, it will ultimately be known as a 10-nation confederacy.

In Daniel's prophecy of the 10 toes, or nations, he said they will be gored by a "little horn" (7:8). This horn, a person, will rule the entire world (Revelation 13:7); and he will be a remarkable individual indeed. The Bible has a good deal to say about him, calling him by different names. John called him "the beast" (Revelation 13:4) and "the antichrist" (1 John 4:3); Paul, "the man of lawlessness" (2 Thessalonians 2:3). Other writers gave him other names. The Apocalypse points out that the 10-toe federation ruled over by this

"There will arise 'the man.' He will be strong in action, epigrammatic in manner, personally handsome, and continuously victorious. He will sweep aside parliaments and demagogues, carry civilizations to glory, reconstruct them into an empire, and hold it together by circulating his profile and organizing further successes. He will codify everything, galvanize Christianity; he will organize learning into meek academies of little men and prescribe a wonderful educational system, and the grateful nations will deify a lucky and progressive egotism."

He will have personal charm. The Antichrist will be looked upon as a superman, and the world will worship him. His phenomenal rise to power, his military genius, and his exploits will be nothing short of spectacular and colossal. Further, he will be a public speaker par excellence and will sway the world with his "mouth speaking great things" (Daniel 7:8, KJV). John says he will have a "mouth like that of a lion" (Revelation 13:2), probably suggesting strength and authority in what he says.

As you read other apocalyptic passages about his words, you will note that much of his speech is against God, or the Lord Jesus, or the saints. For example: "The beast was given a mouth to utter proud words and blasphemies" (Revelation 13:5). "He opened his mouth to blaspheme God, and to slander his name and his dwelling place, and those who live in heaven" (13:6).

Life in the Tribulation

Today's sophisticated man is prone to make the Tribulation so far removed from himself that it has the appearance of "another world." However, such will not actually be the case. The Tribulation will take place right here on earth, probably among people living today. After the Rapture, the Tribulation will begin; and though it is to last only seven years, there will probably be a gradual transition into the last three and one-half years, which Christ referred to as "great tribulation" (Matthew 24:21, KJV). During the Tribulation cars will be bought and sold, roads will be built, and crops will be planted and harvested. In general, life will continue as usual except that the world will be much more <u>materialistic</u> and <u>violent.</u> It will be a horrible time.

Satan will rule the world. Crime will skyrocket, and Satan worship will be worldwide (see Revelation 13). Morals will drop even lower, and God will be publicly attacked (Revelation 13:6). Besides, judgments of God will be poured out on the earth. What a terrible time awaits an unregenerate world!

Worship During the Tribulation

Perhaps much of today's public worship will go on as usual the Sunday following the Rapture, since many give only lip service to Christ. Many professing Christians deny numerous facets of the faith, such as the virgin birth of Christ, the regeneration Jesus offers, the return of Christ in the Rapture, and the inspiration of His Holy Word.

Some people simply go to church because they long for fellowship with God, and church attendance somehow appeases that yearning. Yet they have never repented of their sins and accepted Christ into their lives. They may be religious and moral and have some knowledge of Christ, but they have never been made a new creature in Christ.

Since Christ is not returning for merely good people but for those who truly know Him, He will leave all who are unregenerate here. Many of those left will go to church the following Sunday, probably with renewed interest in the spiritual side of life. Ultimately, however, they will be forced to worship Satan or die (Revelation 13).

The Apostate Church

Have you ever wondered about the plain language used in Revelation 17, where it speaks of "the great prostitute"? That disreputable woman is God's way of describing by use of symbolic language the world religion during the first half of the Tribulation. Even today there is a strong move in many quarters to amalgamate all denominations into a super-world church. Some years ago Dr. Henry P. Van Dusen said, "To an age destined to survive, if at all, as 'one world,' we bring the beginnings of a united church." Dr. J.V. Langmead-Casserly, an Episcopal theologian, predicted that by the turn of the century there will be "a great united church under the leadership of a reinterpreted papacy."

Concerning the coming world church, Charles H. Stevens, writing in the book *Prophecy and the Seventies*, predicted: "There will be the establishment of one world religion . . . on the concept of the universal Fatherhood of God and brotherhood of man."

The world church, being completely apostatized, will be altogether divorced from the principles of faith held today by the Christian church. The Bible refers to this world religion symbolically as Babylon. For years a world church has been discussed. It was considered in 1910 during the World Conference on Missionary Cooperation at Edinburgh. Many of the church leaders involved in today's World Council of Churches are liberalistic, and liberalism has long denied the deity of Christ and His second coming.

Just as the ecumenical church of today appears to be laying the foundation for the apostate church of the Tribulation, so communism in its day helped to lay the groundwork for the form of unbelief that will result in a world religion in which God will be completely forsaken. Then man will worship Satan in the person of the Antichrist during the latter half of the Tribulation (Revelation 13:4). Today Satan is openly worshiped by many in America. Satan uses witchcraft and mind-expanding drugs, among other things, to pull attention to himself.

Some habitual users of drugs will tell you that they know there is a devil, for they have seen him. A contemporary so-called witch said, "We worship a horned god, the prince of darkness, and this makes some people say we are devil-worshipers." All of these things are forerunners of the type of satanic worship that will be the state religion during the Tribulation (Revelation 13:15).

Obviously, the church structure remaining after the Rapture will be without the people of God. Its ministry will not know God, and its theology will ignore God's Word. Such an organization is destined to suffer the judgment of the Almighty. The Bible presents this apostate church symbolically as a prostitute, a wicked woman, riding a scarlet beast (Revelation 17). Though the beast (the Antichrist) is the world ruler (Revelation 13), the church is riding him, signifying the power of the church.

Apparently, the apostate church and the Antichrist will make an alliance and will move into complete world power together (Revelation 17:3, 7). However, when Antichrist no longer needs the apostate church, he will destroy it (Revelation 17:16). In fact, God leads him to do so (v. 17).

Then the Antichrist will set up his own worship system

(note how often the word *worship* is used in Revelation 13), and during the last three and a half years of the Tribulation, Satan worship will be the state religion. In fact, this seems to be the reason for taking the mark of the Beast. The mark will probably give testimony that the people acknowledge the Antichrist as god. The Scriptures state, "He was given power to . . . cause all who refused to worship the image to be killed" (v. 15).

Conversions During the Tribulation

In his book *The Bible and Tomorrow's News*, Charles C. Ryrie states his conviction that the six seal judgments of God (Revelation 6:1-17) will probably take place on earth during the first year of the Tribulation, the first seal (conquest) in the first few months. He thinks the second seal (war) and the third (famine) will closely follow. Incidentally Ryrie, along with some other scholars, thinks that the seven-year Tribulation does not necessarily start the day after the Rapture. He says there may be a time lapse and points out that not the Rapture but the Antichrist's making a seven-year pact with Israel (Daniel 9:27) marks the beginning of that holocaust.

During this time of God's judgment upon a Satan-controlled world, people will be converted. A group of 144,000 zealous evangelists, who themselves will have turned to God after the Rapture (Revelation 7:4), will proclaim God's righteousness. The ecumenical world church will oppose this strong witness and will, in the name of religion, kill people for their faith. The Bible says this apostate church will be "drunk with the blood of the saints, the blood of those who bore testimony to Jesus" (Revelation 17:6).

Hal Lindsey says that the 144,000 will evangelize with

the zeal of Billy Graham. Think of evangelists scattering throughout the world proclaiming the redeeming grace of God. The Bible gives the results of their labor: "After this I looked and there before me was a great multitude that no one could count, from every nation, tribe, people and language, standing before the throne and in front of the Lamb. They were wearing white robes and were holding palm branches in their hands. . . . 'These are they who have come out of the great tribulation; they have washed their robes and made them white in the blood of the Lamb'" (Revelation 7:9, 14).

This reference gives two facts: (1) Many will turn to the Lord during the Tribulation, and (2) thousands upon thousands will be slaughtered because of their faith.

The Two Witnesses

The two witnesses of Revelation 11 stand out like the Rock of Gibraltar in the turbulent sea of world conflict. Note the record: "These men have power to shut up the sky so that it will not rain during the time they are prophesying; and they have power to turn the waters into blood and to strike the earth with every kind of plague as often as they want. Now when they have finished their testimony, the beast that comes up from the Abyss will attack them, and overpower and kill them" (Revelation 11:6, 7).

Though some students believe these two men will live during the latter half of the Tribulation, scholars such as Pentecost, Walvoord, Biederwolf, and others place them in the first. It seems that they will appear before the "abomination that causes desolation" (Matthew 24:15), which will take place in the middle of the Tribulation. Some think that Antichrist will slay the witnesses, destroy the apostate church, and break his covenant with Israel rapidly—in that order. But until God permits it, the Antichrist can do nothing with the two unusual witnesses.

Like the Old Testament prophets who called down fire, they will have power to destroy their adversaries with fire. They will turn water to blood, bring plagues, and prevent rain. These two saints will cause no little annoyance to the Antichrist and his cohorts when they decide to invoke a worldwide drought, causing great devastation, along with the other disasters visiting the earth.

Various opinions have been offered concerning the identity of these witnesses, including Moses and Elijah or Enoch and Elijah. However, others feel that we cannot know who they will be. W.A. Criswell, writing in his *Expository Sermons on Revelation*, Volume 4, said, "I have one suggestion to make about their identification and it is this: from every syllable that is written here in the Word, I would think they are men, they are persons. . . . We do not know who they are. We shall have to wait and see."

Death of the Witnesses

The Bible says that "when they have finished their testimony," the Antichrist will slay the two witnesses. The great problems they will cause this world ruler is indicated by his vindictive actions after their death. We do not know what weapon is used to murder the witnesses, but once they are killed, "their bodies will lie in the street of the great city . . . three and a half days" (Revelation 11:8, 9). And the Antichrist will not allow them to be buried! Apparently these two preachers will have been a great annoyance to many people. Antichrist will probably declare a holiday. The people will rejoice and send each other gifts.

As long as the witnesses' bodies lie in the street, the whole world will be able to see them (v. 9), thanks to television and satellites. Feeling that they have destroyed the last vestige of righteousness, no doubt some will make quick transoceanic flights to Jerusalem to see the bodies and to celebrate. If they had believed the preaching of the witnesses, they would be sad instead of rejoicing.

However, there will be worldwide dismay in the middle of the fourth day: "A breath of life from God entered them, and they stood on their feet" (v. 11). While the world watches, the two decaying bodies will come to life, stand up, and ascend to heaven in answer to a "loud voice," which the world may also hear via microphones and television. Imagine all of this happening in a day of Satan worship and almost total denial of God. This is not all that transpires that day. An earthquake centered in Jerusalem will kill thousands. Then the people will be afraid and will give glory "to the God of heaven" (v. 13).

The Great Tribulation

After Antichrist has killed the two witnesses, he will destroy the apostate church and break his seven-year contract with the Jews, signaling the beginning of the last three and a half years of the period, known as the Great Tribulation. A world war will develop, and armies will gather for the Battle of Armageddon, which Christ will end with His triumphant return to earth. Those events we will discuss in the next chapter.

The discussion in this chapter of the first three and a half years of the Tribulation is not intended to be exhaustive, but rather an overview of that period with a close look at some of the events prophesied. With the two witnesses in mind and all the others through the centuries who have given their lives for their faith, I end this chapter with the following poem:

> I saw the martyr at the stake,
> The flames could not his courage shake,
> Nor death his soul appall.
> I asked him whence his strength was given,
> He looked triumphantly to heaven
> And answered, "Christ is all."
>
> *—Author Unknown*

CHAPTER 8

The GREAT TRIBULATION

The world is headed for upheaval and destruction of catastrophic proportions. A time is coming when more than half of the earth's population will die within a few years time. If this sounds like the talk of a prophet of doom, it is meant to, for that is exactly what awaits the world—doom.

The Bible repeatedly divides the seven-year Tribulation into two equal parts and stresses that the latter half will be nearly unbearable. It is understandable that Jesus, when referring to those horrendous days of the latter half, called them a time of "great distress." He said that unless those times were shortened, all mankind would perish.

The prophet Jeremiah called it "a time of trouble for Jacob" (30:7), Ezekiel named the period a furnace for melting Israel (22:19-22); Daniel spoke of it as "a time of distress" (12:1), Joel referred to those days as "a day of darkness and gloom" (2:2), and Jesus admonished people to pray that they might be able to escape that period (Luke 21:36).

In the Book of Revelation, 14 chapters (6-19) are devoted to the subject. Also Jesus spared no words in describing it: "Those will be days of distress unequaled from the beginning, when God created the world, until now—and never to be equaled again" (Mark 13:19).

The Last Half

Both Testaments emphasize the two halves of the Tribulation, dividing each into exactly three and a half years. Daniel divided the period by pointing out incidents "in the middle of that 'seven'" (9:27; see also 12:7), while the Apocalypse refers to "a time, times and half a time" (Revelation 12:14).

The Bible declares that the length of each period will be 42 months (Revelation 11:2; 13:5), and other references give the number of the days as being 1,260 (Revelation 11:3; 12:6). Even though the Tribulation is divided into two parts, the parts are closely integrated, making up a whole (Daniel 9:27). Hence, they are not two periods separated by a span of time, but the latter immediately follows the former.

You will remember our looking at some predicted events that evidently will happen during the first half of the Tribulation. It is believed that in the beginning the Antichrist will secure his position by pulling world powers to himself. Understandably, he will try to crush those who refuse to cooperate.

Also, during the first three and a half years the apostate church will be a close ally of the Antichrist, and it will have great influence over him (Revelation 17:3). Amazingly, in the midst of all this, the two witnesses (Revelation 11) will

THE GREAT TRIBULATION

minister and will turn thousands to God and be a general hindrance to the Antichrist.

As you read the scriptural account of the events leading up to the end of the first half of the Tribulation, you will see that apparently things will begin to happen in quick succession. Russia, whatever her formation at that time, will fall (Ezekiel 39:4-6); the apostate church will be crushed (Revelation 17:16); and the two witnesses will be killed. When these things happen the Antichrist will usher in the last three and a half years of the Tribulation when he sets up "the abomination that causes desolation" (see Daniel 9:27; 11:31).

The Abomination That Causes Desolation

Jesus, quoting Daniel, referred to a grave breach of Jewish worship which will take place in the middle of the Tribulation. He said, "So when you see standing in the holy place 'the abomination that causes desolation,' spoken of through the prophet Daniel—let the reader understand—then let those who are in Judea flee to the mountains" (Matthew 24:15, 16).

Satan, who will instigate the activities of the Antichrist (Revelation 13:2), has always wanted to be worshiped. He even tried to get Christ to worship him during the wilderness temptation. Therefore, with the apostate church out of the way and the two witnesses murdered, he will have a free hand in religious matters. This is when he will break his agreement with Israel and will blatantly demand that Israel and the rest of the world worship him on penalty of death (Revelation 13:12, 15).

The apostle Paul spoke of that event: "Don't let anyone deceive you in any way, for that day will not come until the rebellion occurs and the man of lawlessness is revealed, the man doomed to destruction. He opposes and exalts himself over everything that is called God or is worshiped, and even sets himself up in God's temple, proclaiming himself to be God" (2 Thessalonians 2:3, 4).

Notice that Paul said the Antichrist will seat himself in the Jewish Temple, the place of worship which Israel highly reveres. This godless man will be brashly proclaiming that he is God. This gross sacrilege will fulfill the prediction of the abomination of desolation, which is a desecration of the Temple by a Gentile's entering the holy place. The Holy Place was a section of the Temple that only an authorized priest was allowed to enter. Such an abomination occurred another time, when in 165 B.C. a conqueror by the name of Antiochus Epiphanes actually slaughtered a swine in the Holy Place. However, this act did not completely fulfill Daniel's prediction; that will happen when Antichrist reigns.

Some Jews Escape

When reading such references as Revelation 3:10, 7:9-14; 13:7, 8 and Isaiah 34:2, you find it evident that the Tribulation will be worldwide in scope. Though this is a fact, that seven-year period is spoken of in the Bible especially in relation to Israel (see Daniel 9:24 and Matthew 24). God told Daniel that the time was decreed for his people and his holy city. Therefore, the Jews are in focus at the time of the Tribulation, though the whole world is included also. Jesus, addressing the Jews, said that when they see the Antichrist desecrate the Temple, "let those who are in Judea flee to the mountains" (Matthew 24:16). Of course, the reason for fleeing will be to escape the wrath of the Satan-directed Antichrist.

THE GREAT TRIBULATION

It is worth mentioning here that the ancient area of Petra is located in the hills about 50 miles south of the Dead Sea. Enclosed by sandstone cliffs brightly veined with varied shades of red, purple, and yellow, this site of earlier civilizations, dating back thousands of years, is approached from the east through a narrow gorge nearly a mile and a half long. Though at times people reside there, it was occupied for hundreds of years only by wandering tribesmen. Many Bible scholars believe this to be the area that God has preserved for those Jews who will escape the Antichrist. Petra is located in biblical Moab, and the Scriptures state that the land of Moab "will be delivered from his [Antichrist's] hand" (Daniel 11:41). The Lord will assist the Jewish people with their escape to the wilderness (Revelation 12:6, 13, 14); and when Antichrist sets out to destroy them, a great earthquake will wipe out that portion of his forces (v. 16).

Apostate World Ruler

Demanding to be worshiped, the Antichrist will curse God, the house of worship, and the raptured saints. Revelation states: "He opened his mouth to blaspheme God, and to slander his name and his dwelling place and those who live in heaven" (13:6). This Anti-God world leader will do all within his power to tear down every vestige of worship of the Trinity. Clyde C. Cox comments in his *Apocalyptic Commentary*: "The beast is an atheist.... To promulgate his atheistic claim, he will be antagonistic toward any mode of worship or place of worship, even the tabernacles or church houses. The name of our God or of our Lord Jesus Christ will become the target of his persecution; he will curse the name of God." Daniel says that he "will say unheard-of things" (11:36).

Robbing Israel of the choice to worship God (Daniel 9:27), Antichrist instead will demand that Israel and the whole earth actually worship him. Note how often the word *worship* is used in Revelation 13 in reference to the Antichrist. Quite likely, the badge of allegiance of worship to him will be the mark of the Beast (Revelation 13:16, 17). If one does not take the mark, he cannot buy or sell. Hence, the ultimatum will be "Worship me or starve!"

Horrid times will exist on the earth during the Great Tribulation, brought on partly by man's inhumanity to man and partly as direct judgment from God. During this trial of mankind, a portion of Jewry will accept Christ as King; also, many Gentiles will receive Christ and go into the millennial kingdom. Mostly, however, the judgments of God will show up the wantonness of practically all the world which, though under severe trial, will curse God, openly defying Him (Revelation 16:9).

The seal judgments are discussed in Revelation 6. When the seventh seal is opened (8:1), a silence of 30 minutes covers heaven as all of God's celestial beings anticipate the dreadful times to follow upon earth. The seventh seal judgment in turn introduces the trumpet judgments (8:7—9:21; 11:15-19), the last three of which are apparently even harsher than the others.

The Trumpet Judgments

The first trumpet (Revelation 8:7). Evangelical commentators take this reference literally. It states that a third of earth, trees, and grass will be ruined by hail and fire raining down, mingled with blood. This terrible judgment is reminiscent of the Egyptian plagues of the Old Testament. This will be a horrible time, but it is only the introduction of worse devastation to follow.

The second trumpet (vv. 8, 9). This judgment destroys a third of the world's shipping, and a third of the sea turns to blood, killing a third of sea life. What an awful time when God's mercy turns to wrath!

The third trumpet (vv. 10, 11). With this judgment a third of the fresh water of the world is polluted by some sort of mass from outer space entering the atmosphere, understandably burning, and probably causing a fallout problem that somehow affects the drinking water. So severe is this problem of poisoning that "many people died from the waters."

The fourth trumpet (vv. 12, 13). Whereas the first three trumpets had to do with the earth and sea, this judgment deals with the heavens. In speaking of the Tribulation, Jesus foretold "signs in the sun, moon and stars . . ." (Luke 21:25). Now, here in Revelation, John declares that a third of the sun, moon, and stars will be darkened. Progressively, devastation is brought upon the earth in the following order: (1) food is destroyed, (2) shipping is hampered, (3) usable water is limited, and (4) production is hindered.

In his work *The Revelation of Jesus Christ*, John F. Walvoord observed: "The four trumpets deal with aspects of the physical world which are taken more or less for granted. . . . [However] so dramatic are the judgments and so unmistakable an evidence of the power and sovereignty of God that blaspheming men on earth can no longer ignore the fact that God is dealing with them."

The fifth trumpet (9:1-12). This is also called the first woe. It is more severe than the foregoing trumpet judgments. Described in Revelation 9, this first woe has to do with hordes of demons in the likeness of stinging scorpions released from hell to sting people for five months. "They were told not to harm the grass of the earth or any plant or

END TIMES

tree, but only those people who did not have the seal of God on their foreheads. They were not given power to kill them, but only to torture them for five months. And the agony they suffered was like that of the sting of a scorpion when it strikes a man. During those days men will seek death, but will not find it; they will long to die, but death will elude them" (Revelation 9:4-6).

John continues to discuss these spirit beings through verse 11, carefully describing their fierce physical appearance. These scorpions will sting everybody except the redeemed. Their sting is almost unbearable; the pain will be so frightening that people would rather die. However, they will not be able to do so for five months, probably because they will be under the power of the demons, thus being unable to exercise their own will in committing suicide.

Hundreds of years before Patmos, Joel foretold the coming of these same creatures (2:1-10), saying that "they climb into the houses; like thieves they enter through the windows" (v. 9). Such a hellish creature as this is difficult to imagine, but we have no reason to give this scriptural account anything but a literal interpretation. Though some people today do not believe that the devil exists, men then will believe these demon beings from Satan are real when they are painfully stung for five months. No doubt, brilliant scientists will quickly prepare "a sure-kill" pesticide, but these little beings will not be affected, because men cannot kill a demon.

Half of Mankind Dies

The sixth trumpet (9:13ff.). The term woe in the Scriptures refers to some great calamity which is usually a judgment from God. The second woe, which is the sixth trumpet judgment described by John, is introduced by reminding us that "the first woe is past; two other woes are yet to come" (Revelation 9:12). Revelation 9:13-15 implies that this devastating second woe comes about partially as an answer to the prayers of persecuted followers of God. Four angels are released at a set time, and their task it is to slay one-third of mankind.

These four angels may be evil spirits whom God permits to be loosed. The judgment is one of the most far-reaching judgments that takes place during the Tribulation. The death of these millions plus those killed earlier in the fourth seal (Revelation 6:7, 8) adds up to the death of half the world's population within a short time.

Commenting on this second woe, Hal Lindsey stated in his book *The Late Great Planet Earth*: "Immediately after their release an incredible army emerges from the Euphrates . . . it numbers 200 million (Revelation 9:16). . . . They will wipe out a third of the earth's population (Revelation 9:18) . . . by fire, smoke (or air pollution), and brimstone (or melted earth). . . . Many Bible expositors believe that this is an accurate first-century description of a 20th century thermonuclear war."

The Vial Judgments

The third woe which John announced has to do with the very end of the age, known also as the seventh trumpet of judgment (Revelation 11:14-19). This time has to do, in part, with voices from heaven announcing in unison: "The kingdom of this world has become the kingdoms of our Lord and of his Christ, and he will reign for ever and ever" (v. 15). However, before Christ returns and sets up His reign, Revelation's seven bowl or vial judgments must take place. These incredibly horrible times may come within the last few months or even the last weeks of the Tribulation.

Those will be days of inconceivable hardship. For thousands of years our loving Father has withheld judgment that wicked men deserved. Now He will delay no longer, for mankind will have fully demonstrated that it has absolutely no intention of honoring or obeying God (9:20, 21).

The first vial (16:2) brings "ugly and painful sores . . . on the people who had the mark of the beast." Only those who have not taken the mark of the Beast will escape this plague.

The second vial (v. 3) turns the seas to blood, killing every living thing in them, and doubtlessly sending up an unbearable stench on seacoasts around the world. Whereas the second trumpet judgment turned one-third of the sea to blood, this second vial judgment appears to affect all seas. Seventy-two percent of the earth's surface is water, and it is easy to understand the devastating effect of this plague.

The third vial (vv. 4-7) turns the fresh water of the world into blood. Just as evil men have shed the blood of countless "saints and prophets," God now gives them "blood to drink as they deserve" (v. 6). In this reference the angel justifies God's judgments, saying, "Yes, Lord God Almighty, true and just are your judgments" (v. 7). Thousands upon thousands of God's followers will be killed during the Tribulation, and this plague will be in retribution for that bloodletting.

The fourth vial (vv. 8, 9) intensifies the heat of the sun so that men will be "seared by the intense heat" (v. 9), yet John says "they cursed the name of God . . . [and] they refused to repent and glorify him." You may know people who believe that wicked men would repent if they were brought

THE GREAT TRIBULATION

under the direct judgment of God, and perhaps some of them would, but these accounts of the last days demonstrate that wicked men will curse God at the end time during judgment.

The fifth vial (vv. 10, 11) deals with the very capital of the world ruler, along with the entire world. Like some of the plagues of Egypt, this judgment brings darkness, sores, and intense pain. The Bible says, "Men gnawed their tongues in agony" (v. 10), and they blasphemed God because of their extreme suffering.

The sixth vial (vv. 12-16) dries up the Euphrates river which has recently been turned to blood. Isaiah 11:15 predicts the drying up of the Euphrates. This permits passage across the riverbed "for the kings from the East" (Revelation 16:12) as they go to Palestine to fight in the battle of Armageddon (v. 14). These kings are apparently oriental, coming from countries such as China and others.

The seventh vial (vv. 17-21) is accompanied by the announcement "It is done!" (v. 17), meaning that the end has come. The destruction that then breaks loose is incredible. Note what happens (vv. 18-21): (1) flashes of lightening, rumblings, peals of thunder; (2) a severe earthquake, apparently making shambles of all world capitals. Besides, every island sinks, and mountains crumble; (3) hailstones weighing 100 pounds batter the earth. Little wonder that Jesus said if those days were not shortened, nobody could survive!

Are you tempted to say that these hideous things could never happen, that these scriptural references are some sort of symbolism and are not to be taken literally? If so, remember that God has done some of these very things before when He sent the 10 plagues on Egypt millennia ago

END TIMES

(Exodus 7–12). At that time God turned water to blood, caused sores, hail, locusts, and darkness. God has lost none of His power. Therefore, at the end of this age He will again carry out plagues such as fell on Egypt, except this time they will be much more severe and will affect the whole earth.

Campaign of Armageddon

While the judgments of God are being poured out upon the world, man's inhumanity to man will add additional misery. For example, it may well be that such atrocities as were committed at Hitler's Buchenwald and Dachau will be repeated many times over, carried out by Antichrist and his godless forces. Also, it seems that war will rage during the last half of the Tribulation.

It has been commonly believed that Armageddon will be a single battle lasting only a few days, but that does not seem to be what the Bible actually says. It states that spirits of hell will gather the kings of the earth "for the battle on the great day of God Almighty" (Revelation 16:14). The account continues: "Then they gathered the kings together to the place that in Hebrew is called Armageddon" (v. 16).

In his book titled *Things to Come*, J. Dwight Pentecost explains: "The extent of this great movement in which God deals with the kings of the earth and of the whole world (Revelation 16:14) will not be seen unless it is realized that the battle of that great day of God Almighty (Revelation 16:14) is not an isolated battle, but rather a campaign that extends over the last half of the Tribulation period. The Greek word *polemos*, translated 'battle' in Revelation 16:14, signifies a war or campaign." Many Bible scholars think that the Battle (campaign) of Armageddon will last throughout the last three and a half years of the Tribulation.

THE GREAT TRIBULATION

At the surrender of Japan, which ended World War II, General Douglas MacArthur said: "If we do not devise some greater and more equitable system, Armageddon will be at our door." He knew the holocaust of war, and he feared it. Yet, we have not found that more equitable system, and there is a constant fear of a global conflict. In 1967 former President Eisenhower said that unless peace can be negotiated, then Armageddon will soon follow, and President Kennedy stated, "Mankind must put an end to war, or war will put an end to mankind." This final, global war that politicians fear is graphically described in the Bible.

As has been pointed out, Armageddon will be a campaign, not a single battle; and the nations will be called together by Satan to fight it. Though the nations come together at the instigation of the devil, God will deal with the armies of the world because of their mistreatment of Israel (Joel 3:2), because of their great wrongdoings (Revelation 19:15), and because of their utter godlessness (16:9).

War in Palestine

The armies of the world will be summoned to a place "that in Hebrew is called Armageddon" (Revelation 16:16). Armageddon is sometimes rendered *Har-Megiddo, har* meaning "mountain," and *megiddo* meaning "slaughter." Megiddo is in the Holy Land. It will be amazing to see all the armies of the earth converging on Palestine. Years ago the prophet Joel wrote of that day: "Proclaim this among the nations: Prepare for war! Rouse the warriors! Let all the fighting men draw near and attack. Beat your plowshares into swords and your pruning hooks into spears. Let the weakling say, 'I am strong!' Come quickly, all you nations from every side, and assemble there. 'Bring down your warriors, O Lord! Let the nations be roused; let them advance into the Valley of Jehoshaphat, for then I will sit to judge all the nations on every side'" (Joel 3:9-12). God speaking through Zechariah said, "I will gather all nations to Jerusalem to fight against it . . ." (14:2). In his book *Expository Sermons on Revelation*, volume 5, W.A. Criswell commented: "These armies will be converging on Palestine. Enemies will gather from every side. It will be a war to exterminate Israel; it will be a war of nation against nation; and it will be a war against God."

As I rode across the plain of Megiddo, the site of Armageddon, some years ago, I tried to imagine the magnitude of the coming final campaign of the ages that is to take place there. While musing on the conflagration, I remembered the plain is 14 by 20 miles in size and is one of the most natural battlefields in all the world. Thousands of years ago Thothmes III of Egypt said, "Megiddo is worth a thousand cities," and Napoleon allegedly remarked that it was the most ideal location on earth for a battle. Personally, I have never seen an "ideal" location for a battle!

Armageddon Widespread

The great military campaign of the end times will include several battles and will probably take place over an extended period of time. Besides Megiddo, there is to be a battle in the valley of Jehosaphat (Joel 3:2), which seems to be an area east of Jerusalem. Also, in two different chapters, Isaiah speaks of conflict coming from Edom, or Idumea, which is south of Jerusalem (see Isaiah 34; 63.) Further, Jerusalem is graphically described as the site of conflict (Zechariah 12:2-11; 14:2, 3). Therefore, it seems evident that

THE GREAT TRIBULATION

the campaign will extend from Megiddo on the north to Edom on the south, thus covering almost all of Palestine and, quite likely, other countries of the Middle East as well.

It appears that during the latter half of the Tribulation, Antichrist will have his headquarters in Palestine (Daniel 11:45) and the armies of the East will invade and attack his forces (Revelation 16:12-16). The Western powers, quite probably including the United States, may be on the side of Antichrist. The nations of the South will be involved also. Russia will have been destroyed earlier in fulfillment of Ezekiel 38; 39. Though the Soviet Union has undergone great change, the Bible's prediction of Russia's attacking Israel is yet to be fulfilled. Some Bible students believe that Russia's invasion of Palestine and her subsequent destruction at the middle of the Tribulation will trigger the Armageddon campaign, which will last throughout the last three and a half years of the Tribulation.

A Summary

When we look at what the Bible says about the end time, we find it frightening indeed. With mass media coverage of world events, television sets around the world will be giving out the awful news in ghastly detail as one event after another takes place, including the judgments of God as well as the Battle (campaign) of Armageddon.

In summing up the military conflicts of that day, the following seems to be the order: (1) The armies of the southern nations are defeated (mentioned in Daniel 11:40). (2) Russia and her allies invade Israel and are destroyed by God (Ezekiel 38; 39). (3) Antichrist breaks his pact with Israel and then occupies the Holy Land (Daniel 11:41-45); thus, with the northern confederacy and the confederacy of the southern nations out of the way, the massive armies of the East are the only threat to Antichrist and his forces. (4) Then these Asiatic powers invade Palestine (Revelation 16:14) in preparation for the climatic battle of the Tribulation.

Sign in the Sky

In His Olivet Discourse, Christ discussed the very last days of the Tribulation. He said: "At that time the sign of the Son of Man will appear in the sky . . ." (Matthew 24:30), implying that some phenomenon will occur in the sky just before He returns. We do not know what the sign will be, but the Scriptures do reveal man's reaction to it. The armies of the East and those of Antichrist will forget their differences and will give their sole attention to the heavens, apparently trying to blast Christ out of the sky. John declares, "Then I saw the beast and the kings of the earth and their armies gathered together to make war against the rider on the horse and his army" (Revelation 19:19; see also Zechariah 14:3; Revelation 17:14; 19:11-21).

The Second Coming

While the armies of the earth are poised to make war against Christ, He will suddenly burst upon the scene and literally destroy those armies "by the splendor of his coming" (2 Thessalonians 2:8). Evidently, our Lord will employ atomic fission at this time, the secret of which He knew a long time before Einstein ever dreamed of splitting the atom.

You will notice that the Bible describes the terrible day when hordes of Christ's enemies will actually melt away. Zechariah graphically portrays the scene: "Their flesh will rot while they are still standing on their feet, their eyes will

THE GREAT TRIBULATION

rot in their sockets, and their tongues will rot in their mouths" (Zechariah 14:12). The remnant will meet death when they are slain by Christ, and the fowls will eat their flesh (Revelation 19:21).

Christ the King will first touch the earth on the Mount of Olives, the very hill from which He ascended. At that time Olivet will divide, forming a great valley (Zechariah 14:3, 4, 8; Ezekiel 47:8-10).

Our Redeemer will return from heaven as King of kings and Lord of lords (Revelation 19:16), and all of His glorified believers will accompany Him (Jude 14, 15). In quick succession He will destroy the Antichrist and his lieutenant (Revelation 19:20), and He will have Satan bound and cast into the bottomless pit, where he will remain for a thousand years (Revelation 20:1-3). Since no unsaved person can enter the millennial age (Zechariah 13:9; Matthew 25:30, 46), Christ will judge those living upon the earth when the Tribulation ends. The righteous will be admitted into the Millennium, and the wicked will suffer eternal punishment.

Christ, who is the Prince of Peace, will then rule this entire world for a thousand years. Purity of motive, holiness in worship, and universal peace will be as common then as sin, apostasy, and war are today. May God speed that day!

The Earthly Reign of Christ

The thousand-year reign of Christ on earth will break forth like a beautiful, cloudless day after a night of violent storm. Just as the Tribulation will be a period of upheaval, disorder, and destruction, the thousand years following it will be a time of tranquility, order, and peace. That age will be known as the Millennium. The word *millennium* comes from two Latin words meaning "1,000 years," and six times in Revelation 20:1-7 the Bible refers to that blessed and benevolent time.

The Lord Jesus himself will be the world ruler then, and peace will spread around the globe. For 1,000 years there will be almost no sickness, hence no clinics, hospitals, or asylums. Doctors will have to turn to other professions, and pharmaceutical firms will be nonexistent. Funeral parlors will not be common, because sickness and death will be at a minimum. Also, there will be no more war.

Imagine a time when there will be no talk of war! These

END TIMES

days the news media constantly report that some nation is fighting another somewhere, but then neither war nor the awful pain and sorrow which accompany it will exist. Also, violence in the streets and homes will be unknown. Apparently, during the Millennium there will be no jails, no prisons, and no places of teenage detention. Righteousness will reign throughout the earth.

Many people starve to death each year, and it is said that half of the world goes to bed hungry every night. Not so during the blessed Millennium. The Word of God is careful to tell us that everybody will have plenty to eat then. Hunger and famine will be unknown when Christ the Messiah rules the world.

Christ Comes to Earth

Earlier we studied the scriptural account of the Tribulation. The stern judgments of God coupled with the demon-motivated crimes of the Antichrist will make for a time of indescribable pain and sorrow. However, when it looks as though man will be completely annihilated, Christ will return from heaven accompanied by the saints, including you and me. In quick succession He will end the war of Armageddon, cast Antichrist and the False Prophet into hell, judge all living men, have Satan bound and cast into the bottomless pit, and then set up His millennial reign here on earth.

Since Christ's theocratic government will be so utterly different from any system in the world today, comprehension of it does not come easy. He will rule the world from Jerusalem, the same city where He was crucified. His "great society" programs will truly be great, and His holy plans for world peace will really work. What a magnificent day it will be when Jesus rules the earth!

THE EARTHLY REIGN OF CHRIST

Jesus Judges Living Men

Not everyone will be destroyed at Armageddon. Of course, many people will not be involved in that war and will live on after its conclusion. These are the people Christ talked about being judged (Matthew 25:31-46). Concerning that time, the psalmist declared, "For he comes, he comes to judge the earth. He will judge the world in righteousness and the peoples in his truth" (Psalm 96:13); and Luke wrote, "For he has set a day when he will judge the world with justice by the man he has appointed" (Acts 17:31).

Several judgments will take place just before the beginning of the Millennium. Not only will the Antichrist and the False Prophet be judged and cast into hell, and Satan bound and cast into the bottomless pit, but also both the living Jews and the Gentiles will be judged.

Judgment of Jews. Designed to keep rebels out of the Millennium, this judgment will have to do with all Jews alive at that time. Described by the prophet Ezekiel, that judgment will deal with all Jews who survived the Tribulation (Ezekiel 20:37, 38). Jesus referred to that judgment in a parable (Matthew 25:14-30).

In Matthew 24:30, 31 Jesus said that the angels "will gather his elect from the four winds." Matthew 25:30 says that the "worthless servant" will be cast out, but the good and faithful servant will be told to "come and share your master's happiness" (v. 23). Those that are found to belong to God will enter the Millennium in their earthly bodies.

Only the converted will enter the Millennium. Daniel says, "But the saints of the Most High will receive the kingdom and will possess it forever—yes, for ever and ever" (7:18), and he repeats this in verse 22 and also in verse 27. He seems to be emphasizing that no blasphemer, no rejector, no sinner will have any place in the glorious, righteous kingdom. Such persons will be denied admittance to both the kingdom and eternal life (see Ezekiel 20:35-38; Matthew 25:30).

Judgment of Gentiles. Of the more than five billion people in the world today, only about 17.5 million are Jews. If that ratio still exists at the end of the Tribulation, you can readily see that most of the people living will be non-Jews, or Gentiles. Nonetheless, since Jews are the race God chose to work through thousands of years ago in order to win the world, much of the Scripture differentiates between the Jews and the Gentiles right up to and, in fact, through the Millennium.

The Bible speaks of the judgment of the Gentiles who survive the Tribulation. This judgment will take place "when the Son of Man comes in his glory . . . " (Matthew 25:31-46), and it will be upon individuals rather than nations. Some Bible students believe that *Gentiles* is a better translation than *heathen or nations* in this passage. The individual non-Jews will be judged on the basis of their regeneration, just as the Jews will be.

Treatment of the Brethren

It seems that the criterion for acceptance at this judgment will rest upon treatment of "these brothers of mine" (Matthew 25:40), apparently speaking of the Jews of the Tribulation. The lines will be so emphatically drawn during the Tribulation that apparently the only reason a Gentile will befriend the persecuted Jew will be due to the Gentile's love and acceptance of God. In other words, it seems that only born-again people will help the born-again Jew during the last half of the Tribulation. If the Gentile feeds, clothes,

THE EARTHLY REIGN OF CHRIST

or visits the Jew (see Matthew 25:35, 36), he will do so at the risk of his very life, and he will not do that unless the love of God dwells in his heart.

The Gentiles who are thus found to have experienced the new birth will be admitted to the kingdom (Matthew 25:34). Those who opposed God's people will be denied entrance (v. 41). Just how this judgment will be carried out on Gentiles throughout the world, we are not told. We do know that a great judgment will take place in the valley of Jehoshaphat (Joel 3:2). Surely God's records will show each individual's inner thoughts and intent toward the persecuted Jew, wherever in the world the Gentile lives.

Our Place in That Judgment

The Bible thus points out that only the "sheep" Gentiles will enter the millennial kingdom, while the "goat" Gentiles will be denied admittance and will be sentenced to eternal punishment. Most of us are Gentiles, and if we fail to be born again now (John 3:3), we could be in the very judgment under discussion, for it is possible for it to take place as soon as seven years from now. The born-again person will be raptured by Christ before the Tribulation begins (1 Corinthians 15:52; 1 Thessalonians 4:17), then the Tribulation will run for seven years on the earth (Daniel 9:27), and then this judgment of the living Gentiles will transpire.

You and I will be in one of four positions during this Gentile judgment: (1) Hopefully, we will have gone in the Rapture, lived with Christ in heaven for seven years, returned with Him to the earth, and thus be only a spectator at this judgment. (2) Or we could fail to go in the Rapture, die or be killed as a sinner during the Tribulation, and thus not appear at this judgment, for we would be judged later instead, at the White Throne Judgment after the Millennium. (3) Another possibility is that we could fail to go in the Rapture and then turn completely to Christ during the Tribulation, survive that seven-year bloodbath, and be living and appear in this judgment. (4) Finally, we could miss the Rapture, accept Christ during the Tribulation, and then die. In that case, we would be resurrected before the Millennium begins.

Those who constantly and consciously reject Christ before the Rapture will find it difficult to turn to Him after the Rapture. If a person has any intention of ever being converted to the Lord, he should come to Him now. He should not wait, hoping to accept Him during the trying days of the Tribulation.

The First Resurrection

The Bible bears out that the first resurrection will consist of several phases. The resurrection of our Lord is the beginning of the first resurrection (1 Corinthians 15:23). Then comes the resurrection at the Rapture of all people who died in Christ during the church age (1 Thessalonians 4:16). The third phase of the first resurrection will take place when Christ returns to the earth to set up the Millennium, and it will consist of the saved who died during the Tribulation (Revelation 20:3-5). Many Bible scholars believe the fourth is when the Old Testament saints will rise (see Daniel 12:2; Isaiah 26:19).

There are actually five resurrections referred to in the Scriptures. While the first four phases of the first resurrection will involve those who will receive eternal life, the fifth and final resurrection, known as the second resurrection, will be of the unsaved dead and will take place after the Millennium. These millions upon millions of souls who have died outside of God down through the ages will receive eternal damnation at that time (see Revelation 20:5, 11-14).

Satan Bound

As the way is cleared for Christ's peaceful reign, Satan will be restrained. John wrote: "And I saw an angel coming down out of heaven, having the key to the Abyss and holding in his hand a great chain. He seized the dragon, that ancient serpent, who is the devil, or Satan, and bound him for a thousand years. He threw him into the Abyss, and locked and sealed it over him, to keep him from deceiving the nations anymore until the thousand years were ended" (Revelation 20:1-3).

This thousand-year incarceration of Satan will give the earth peace and tranquility such as it has not known since before the Fall in Eden. The Bible identifies Satan as the "ways of this world" and "the ruler of the kingdom of the air" (Ephesians 2:2), but the day will come when he will be bound and cast into the bottomless pit. Then after being released for a short while at the end of the Millennium, he will be cast into the lake of fire where he will stay throughout eternity.

The Three Views

Before taking a look at the magnificent Millennium, mention should be made here of the three schools of thought about the thousand-year period. The viewpoints are known as the postmillennial, the amillennial, and the premillennial.

The *postmillenarian* believes that the church will finally overcome evil, hence the world will become better and better. This world will finally become the kingdom of God, it is taught, and the Kingdom will last for 1,000 years, followed by the return of Christ to the earth. Though this doctrine was quite popular in other years, two world wars, a constant worsening of world conditions, and the decline of Christian influence in world society has caused this position to be less popular than formerly.

The *amillenarian* does not believe that there is to be an earthly Millennium either by man improving himself or by the return of Christ. Rather, he teaches that Christ will continue to convert man to Himself until the world comes to an end. At that time Christ will return and carry out a general resurrection and a general judgment. The judgment will separate the redeemed from the lost. The amillenarian, like the postmillenarian, does not take the prophetic Scriptures literally, but rather applies the so-called spiritual interpretation.

The *premillenarian* knows that at times the Bible speaks in symbols; nonetheless, he believes that the Bible should be taken literally unless it is evident that a passage has another interpretation. In other words, he asks, "If the passage makes sense, why seek some other sense?" Most of us are premillennialists. We expect Christ to come in the Rapture, and this event to be followed by the Tribulation, after which Christ will return to the earth and set up His 1,000-year reign. Since we believe that Christ must return before the Millennium, we are called premillennialists.

In summation, then, the postmillenarian believes that Christ will return after the Millennium, the amillenarian does not believe that there will be a Millennium, and the

THE EARTHLY REIGN OF CHRIST

premillenarian believes that Christ will return to the earth before the Millennium.

When Jesus came to this earth, He came as "the Lamb that was slain from the creation of the world" (Revelation 13:8); but when He comes the second time, He will not come as a Lamb. He will come as "the Lion of the tribe of Judah" (Revelation 5:5). This coming will be with power, authority, and majesty; and He will reign in splendor and righteousness. Isaiah describes that reign: "And the government will be on his shoulders. And he will be called Wonderful Counselor, Mighty God, Everlasting Father, Prince of Peace" (9:6).

Who Will Repopulate the Earth?

Jesus said that immortals will not marry but will be as angels (Mark 12:25); therefore, the millions of saints who will return with Christ to the earth and go with Him into the Millennium will not multiply. The world's increase in population will come from the people living here upon earth at the beginning of the Millennium.

Because of the absence of germs and disease, and because of the restoration of Old Testament longevity, the earth's population will increase rapidly after the devastating years of the Tribulation. "There shall be no more thence an infant of days, nor an old man that hath not filled his days: for the child shall die an hundred years old; but the sinner being an hundred years old shall be accursed" (Isaiah 65:20, KJV).

If a person is 100 years old, he will be thought of as a child, while if by the time an individual reaches that age he has not committed himself to the Lord, he "shall be accursed," probably meaning that God will not tolerate his sins beyond that age and he will die.

Apparently, some men will live to be nearly 1,000 years old, thus population will grow at an incredible rate. By the end of the thousand years, the earth's populace will be "like the sand on the seashore" (Revelation 20:8).

Immortals During the Millennium

If you and I go with the Lord Jesus in the Rapture, we will return with Him as immortals when he comes to rule the world. Our precise function as immortals during the Millennium has been debated by the church for centuries. Will the immortal mingle freely with the mortal? Will he eat, sleep, and be a member of earth's society? In his *Things to Come*, Dr. J. Dwight Pentecost states his belief: "The essential character of and purpose in the millennium leads to the conclusion that resurrected individuals, although having a part in the millennium, are not on the earth to be subjects of the King's reign."

Commenting on the matter, Dr. Charles C. Ryrie, in his book *The Bible and Tomorrow's News*, states: "Those who, like the church, have resurrection bodies, will not be subject to physical limitations. Nor will they contribute to space, food or governmental problems during the Millennium. On the contrary, they will share in Christ's righteous rule."

Government During Christ's Reign

In His rule of the world, "the Lord will be king over the whole earth. On that day there will be one Lord, and his name the only name" (Zechariah 14:9). Jerusalem will be the world capital (Isaiah 2:3), it will be a city of great glory (Isaiah 24:23), and the Temple will be located there (Isaiah

THE EARTHLY REIGN OF CHRIST

33:20). Ruling with perfect justice, Christ "will not judge by what he sees with his eyes, or decide by what he hears with his ears; but with righteousness he will judge the needy, with justice he will give decisions for the poor of the earth. He will strike the earth with the rod of his mouth; with the breath of his lips he will slay the wicked. Righteousness will be his belt and faithfulness the sash around his waist" (Isaiah 11:3-5).

The Bible speaks of David's rule in the Millennium (Jeremiah 30:9; Ezekiel 37:24, 25). Having been resurrected after the Tribulation along with other Old Testament saints, he will apparently be a regent or prince. Under him nobles and governors will serve (Isaiah 32:1; Jeremiah 30:21). Further, the 12 disciples will rule over the 12 tribes of Israel (Matthew 19:28). Besides these, there will be lesser posts of authority, such as those over 10 cities or five cities (Luke 19:11-19). Also judges will be active, for "I will restore your judges as in days of old, your counselors as at the beginning" (Isaiah 1:26).

Today frustrated statesmen grapple with international problems as they faithfully labor to stave off war. Constantly we are beating our plowshares into swords (Joel 3:2) as our defense expenditures drain our treasuries. This will not be so in the Millennium. Then "they will beat their swords into plowshares and their spears into pruning hooks. Nation will not take up a sword against nation, nor will they train for war anymore" (Micah 4:3).

Righteousness Everywhere

Then it will be popular to be godly and the ungodly will be very much in the minority. Zechariah speaks of the holiness of the kingdom: "On that day HOLY TO THE LORD will be inscribed on the bells of the horses, and the cooking pots in the Lord's house will be like the sacred bowls in front of the altar. Every pot in Jerusalem and Judah will be holy to the Lord Almighty" (Zechariah 14:20, 21).

The Messiah, described as "the sun of righteousness . . . with healing in its wings" (Malachi 4:2), says, "I am bringing my righteousness near, it is not far away" (Isaiah 46:13). Righteousness and peace are the cornerstones of the Millennium, and the people "will live in peaceful dwelling places, in secure homes, in undisturbed places of rest" (32:18). In the Millennium, it can be said in fact, "Love and faithfulness meet together; righteousness and peace kiss each other" (Psalm 85:10).

A man may sin against God during the Millennium, but mankind's behavior will generally be on a much higher level than now, for Satan will not be there to tempt man. If a person is not genuinely righteous, he will be forced to give outward allegiance to Christ, for the Lord will not condone rebellion then.

Animals Not Vicious

Have you noticed how much the Bible says about the animals in the Millennium? They will not be vicious nor carnivorous, and they will be gentle to the point that a child can have a lion for a pet. Isaiah tells us about it: "The wolf will live with the lamb, the leopard will lie down with the goat, the calf and the lion and the yearling together; and a little child will lead them. The cow will feed with the bear . . . and the lion will eat straw like the ox" (11:6, 7). Later, Isaiah talks about the animals again. He says, "The wolf and the lamb will feed together, and the lion will eat straw like the ox" (65:25).

THE EARTHLY REIGN OF CHRIST

Apparently in Eden, Adam and Eve had no reason to fear the animals, for it seems that they were not vicious before the curse. In the Millennium the curse will be lifted, except death; and then "the infant will play near the hole of the cobra, and the young child put his hand into the viper's nest" (Isaiah 11:8).

No Hunger Then

The Bible is explicit concerning the productivity of the earth during the Millennium. The original curse placed upon the plant and animal kingdom will be lifted and the ground will bring forth bountifully. The seasons will be perfect and "the reaper will be overtaken by the plowman and the planter by the one treading grapes" (Amos 9:13). In other words, the crops will be so large that the workers will not be through gathering them before it is time to plant again.

The phenomenon of nature's returning to its former glory means that choking weeds and harmful plants will cease to exist, so will the burning deserts (see Isaiah 11; 35; 43). Note the marvelous promises given by Isaiah: "Then will the eyes of the blind be opened and the ears of the deaf unstopped. Then will the lame leap like a deer, and the mute tongue shout for joy. Water will gush forth in the wilderness and streams in the desert. The burning sand will become a pool, the thirsty ground bubbling springs" (35:5-7).

Conversions in the Millennium

In order for Christ's thousand-year reign to encompass the whole world, it must, of course, include the Gentile as well as the Jew. The non-Jew is promised participation in the kingdom, and many Scripture passages refer to that fact.

Speaking through the prophet Zechariah, Christ said, "Many nations will be joined with the Lord in that day and will become my people. I will live among you and you will know that the Lord Almighty has sent me to you" (2:11).

Like the Jew, the Gentile must be saved to enter the Millennium. Of course, also like the Jew, his children born after the beginning of the Millennium will have to be converted. As you can imagine, for a while after the start of the Millennium, there will be many teenagers who will have been born after the kingdom began. They must be born again individually (Hebrews 11:6; Romans 4:3). However, it will be easy to commit oneself to Christ then, "for the earth will be full of the knowledge of the Lord as the waters cover the sea" (Isaiah 11:9). Little wonder that "he who fails to reach a hundred will be considered accursed" (Isaiah 65:20).

Filled With the Holy Spirit

Though the Millennium will be an earthly kingdom, its most distinguishing quality will be its spirituality. It will be common for men to be filled with the Spirit. Israel is promised the Spirit: "I will put my Spirit in you and you will live, and I will settle you in your own land" (Ezekiel 37:14).

The Spirit's infilling will be exemplified in worship and praise to the Lord by Jews and Gentiles. Men will willingly obey the Messiah's precepts, for they will possess spiritual power and soul transformation (Isaiah 32:15; Ezekiel 39:29). Apparently the Holy Spirit will be poured out "on all people" (Joel 2:28), for it seems that almost everybody will be Spirit-filled.

In contrast to today's spiritual apathy and worldliness, then there will be spiritual fervor, joyful worship, universal knowledge and understanding of holy truth, and an encompassing fellowship of the saints. Holy living and obedience to God will exist everywhere. Such is the behavior of men filled with the Spirit.

Worship During the Millennium

Much adoration will be given to the Lord Jesus during His thousand-year reign. "In that day you will say: 'I will praise you'" Isaiah tells us (12:1). It seems that Isaiah overflows with worship himself as he continues, "With joy you will draw water from the wells of salvation. In that day you will say: 'Give thanks to the Lord, call on his name; make known among the nations what he has done. . . . Sing to the Lord'" (vv. 3-5).

Jeremiah discusses worship also: "There will be heard once more . . . the voices of those who bring thank offerings to the house of the Lord, saying, 'Give thanks to the Lord Almighty, for the Lord is good; his love endures forever.' For I will restore the fortunes of the land as they were before" (33:10, 11). Everybody will worship the Lord then, for Isaiah tells us, "'From one New Moon to another . . . all mankind will come and bow down before me,' says the Lord" (66:23).

A magnificent Temple will stand in Jerusalem, and Ezekiel describes it and the worship there in minute detail (41:1-25). Though men will praise and worship the Lord throughout the earth, the focal point of worship will be the Temple. You will note the discussion of worship as you read Zechariah 14. Once a year all the nations of the earth "will go up year after year to worship the King, the Lord Almighty, and to celebrate the Feast of Tabernacles" (v. 16).

In case a nation, probably through representatives, fails

END TIMES

to worship the Messiah at Jerusalem, that nation will be punished by having no rain upon its crops (v. 17). However, almost everyone will gladly worship the Lord. After receiving a new, spiritual heart (Jeremiah 31:33), the forgiveness of sins (v. 34), and the fullness of the Spirit (Joel 2:28, 29), people around the world will bow down and worship the incomparable Son of God, the Rose of Sharon, the Prince of Peace.

For the duration of His thousand-year reign, the Rose of Sharon will bloom forth in all of His beauty, purity, and magnificence. All the world will bask in the fragrance of His holy rule. Though the world today is sin-sick and ugly, the Lord Jesus, who is "the rose of Sharon" and the "lily of the valleys" (Song of Solomon 2:1), will someday spread righteousness, beauty, and dignity throughout the universe.

Satan Freed

Like an ugly blight spreading across a beautiful rose garden the spirit of Satan will reach throughout the world at the end of the Millennium. Though his freedom will last for only a short period, Satan will cause thousands of people to rally to himself. John tells us, "When the thousand years are over, Satan will be released from his prison" (Revelation 20:7).

This deceiver of man, ever bent on pulling people from God to himself, "will go out to deceive the nations" and "to gather them for battle" (v. 8). It is astounding that many people will join him and come up against Jerusalem to attack that city (v. 9). You and I may well ask why anybody would turn from the righteous and just rule of Christ to the way of Satan. However, the answer may be obvious.

First, only earthly people—"the nations" (v. 8)— will be

THE EARTHLY REIGN OF CHRIST

involved in this rebellion, not the resurrected saints, who will be immortals throughout the Millennium. The uprising implies that many people will be giving Christ outward allegiance, while their hearts will not be righteous. Christ's rule will be just and fair; nonetheless, He will rule with an iron scepter (Revelation 2:27), probably meaning that disobedience will be dealt with summarily. However, when at the end of the Millennium people are given a choice between Satan and Christ, some will turn to Satan.

At the end of His thousand-year reign, it appears that Christ will veil His glory for awhile, and Satan will be permitted to tempt men, thus revealing those who had been giving only feigned obedience to the Lord. As has been pointed out earlier, children will be born throughout the Millennium (Isaiah 11:6, 8; Zechariah 8:5); and those people will have to be born again—that is, they will have to have a spiritual conversion.

A spiritual rebirth will be as essential during the Millennium as it is now. The end-time rebellion clearly points up that fact, demonstrating two things: (1) Man can live in a virtual Garden of Eden, yet his need of a personal conversion to Christ still exists. (2) Though one's environment is righteous, just, and holy, if he fails to personally turn to Christ, he is a rebel at heart and may oppose the Lord under temptation.

Rebels Destroyed

Hundreds of thousands of people will rebel against God and will ally themselves with Satan (Revelation 20:8). However, compared to the billions upon earth then, the rebellion will probably be small. God will act quickly in putting an end to this sinful rebellion. Fire will rain down from heaven (v. 9) and will destroy Satan's army before it strikes.

Then Satan, the chief rebel of the ages, will forever be done away with. Here we come to what may be the major reason that Satan would steer people away from the Book of Revelation, telling them that it is difficult and irrelevant. He wants mankind to believe that he does not even exist, thus giving him free hand to carry on unhindered.

However, God's Holy Word tells us of Satan, and the Book of Revelation reveals his utter defeat. He will not finally triumph, but instead he will be brought to complete despair and shame. He will be "thrown into the lake of burning sulfur, where the Beast and the false prophet had been thrown. They will be tormented day and night for ever and ever" (Revelation 20:10).

Now Satan would rather that I not tell you that. In fact, he would much prefer that the entire world not know his final destiny, and this is one reason that he steers people away from the book which tells them about it. When he is cast into hell, he is not king there, but he himself is "tormented day and night."

Of course, when God destroys the people who allied with Satan at the close of the Millennium, they will die and be punished as are all evil men. With their passing, all unsaved mortals will be dead. Other people left on earth will be dedicated followers of God and are given immortality; they will dwell in the new heaven and earth throughout eternity.

The Great White Throne Judgment

You may well shudder when you read the somber scriptural account of the judgment of all unsaved people since

THE EARTHLY REIGN OF CHRIST

Adam. The magnitude of the parade of resurrected millions upon millions who never turned to God is staggering. Listen to the awful prediction: "Then I saw a great white throne and him who was seated on it. Earth and sky fled from his presence, and there was no place for them. And I saw the dead, great and small, standing before the throne, and books were opened. Another book was opened, which is the book of life. The dead were judged according to what they had done as recorded in the books" (Revelation 20:11, 12).

What a sobering scene! This is when "those who have done evil will rise to be condemned" (John 5:29), of which Jesus spoke, and it is for the dead who "did not come to life until the thousand years were ended" (Revelation 20:5). No saved person will stand before the Great White Throne; only those whose names are not "in the Lamb's book of life" (21:27).

If our unsaved friends and loved ones do not accept the Lord as Savior, they will stand before Him then as the righteous Judge. Nobody fails to meet the Son of God, for all must bow before Him now, honoring Him as Savior and Lord, or meet Him then as Judge. All who appear at the White Throne Judgment are "thrown into the lake of fire" (Revelation 20:15). This judgment is not the same as the judgment seat of Christ, about which we studied earlier. This sober judgment has to do with all the wicked dead of all ages past.

New Heaven and Earth

After the rebellion and the judgment of the unsaved, John "saw a new heaven and a new earth, for the first heaven and the first earth had passed away" (Revelation 21:1).

The earth will be purified by fire. Peter speaks of that fantastic event: "The heavens will disappear with a roar; the elements will be destroyed by fire, and the earth and everything in it will be laid bare. . . . But in keeping with his promise we are looking forward to a new heaven and a new earth, the home of righteousness" (2 Peter 3:10, 13).

Many Bible scholars believe Peter is saying that the atmosphere and earth will not be destroyed by God, but renovated, making them new, pure and untainted by sinful man. In his *World Aflame*, Billy Graham comments, "Whatever is not suited for the new life of the new world will be destroyed. This is what some call the end of the world, but the world will never end. It will only be changed into a better world." God has said, "I am making everything new!" (Revelation 21:5), and He does this by means of fire.

For Ever and Ever

The apostle Paul had a vision of heaven and later commented that he saw things unlawful to utter. He did say on another occasion, "No eye has seen, no ear has heard, no mind has conceived what God has prepared for those who love him" (1 Corinthians 2:9). John gave us a glimpse of life then when he said, "He will wipe every tear from their eyes. There will be no more death or mourning or crying or pain, for the old order of things has passed away" (Revelation 21:4).

It seems evident that throughout eternity we will be busy thinking and doing and participating on a level that our present finite reasoning cannot at all fathom. I am sure that whatever the great mind of Christ has prepared for you and me will be exciting and satisfying. We will spend our eternity with the Lord in worship, in service, and in companionship. What more could our unworthy hearts ask!

Throughout this book we have studied what the Bible says about things to come. We have delved into prophetic utterances, all of which were made hundreds upon hundreds of years ago. We have been amazed to find that many of those biblical predictions are being fulfilled during our lifetime.

In fact, more of God's predictive Word has come to fruition during this generation than was fulfilled during the entire 1900 years between the Cross and this age. It is evident that the end time foretold in the Bible, and about which the church has taught for centuries, is upon us. May Christ help us to stay ready for the return of our Lord.

GOD'S PLAN OF WORLD EVENTS

OLD TESTAMENT	CHURCH AGE	TRIBULATION 7 YEARS	MILLENNIUM 1000 YEARS	NEW HEAVEN AND EARTH

Rapture — Judgment Seat of Christ — Marriage Supper — Second Coming

Great Tribulation

BATTLE OF ARMAGEDDON

BIBLIOGRAPHY

Biederwolf, William Edward. *The Millennium Bible*. Grand Rapids: Baker Book House, 1969.

Britt, George L. *When Dust Shall Sing*. Cleveland, Tenn.: Pathway Press, 1958.

Brooke, Tal. *When the World Will Be As One*. Eugene, Ore.: Harvest House Publishers, Inc., 1989.

Buxton, Clyne W. *Expect These Things*. Old Tappan, N.J.: The Fleming H. Revell Co., 1973.

Buxton, Clyne W. *What About Tomorrow?* Cleveland, Tenn.: Pathway Press, 1974.

Cho, Paul Yonggi. *Daniel*. Lake Mary, Fla.: Creation House, 1990.

Coder, S. Maxwell. *The Final Chapter*. Wheaton, Ill.: Tyndale House, 1984.

Cox, Clyde C. *Apocalyptic Commentary*. Cleveland, Tenn.: Pathway Press, 1959.

Dake, Finis Jennings. *Revelation Expounded*. Tulsa, Okla.: copyright by author, 1931.

DeHaan, Richard M. *Israel and the Nations in Prophecy*. Grand Rapids: Zondervan Publishing House, 1968.

Drake, H.M. *The Plan of God for the Ages*. Cleveland, Tenn.: Pathway Press, 1966.

Dyer, Charles H. *The Rise of Babylon*. Wheaton, Ill.: Tyndale House Publishers, Inc., 1991.

Feinburg, Charles Lee. *Prophecy and the Seventies*. Chicago: Moody Press, 1971.

Goerner, Henry Cornell. *Thus It Is Written*. Nashville, Tenn.: Convention Press, 1959.

Graham, Billy. *World Aflame*. Garden City, N.Y.: Doubleday & Co., Inc., 1965

Grant, George. *The Blood of the Moon*. Brentwood, Tenn.: Wolgemuth and Hyatt, Publishers, Inc., 1991.

Halley, Henry H. *Halley's Bible Handbook*. Grand Rapids: Zondervan Publishing House, 1965.

Hughes, Ray H. *The Order of Future Events*. Cleveland, Tenn.: Pathway Press, 1962.

Hunt, Dave. *Global Peace*. Eugene, Ore.: Harvest House Publishers, 1990.

Jeremiah, David. *Escape the Coming Night*. Dallas: Word Publishing, 1990.

Kac, Arthur W. *The Rebirth of the State of Israel*. Chicago: Moody Press, 1958.

Kah, Gary H. *En Route to Global Occupation*. Lafayette, La.: Huntington House Publishers, 1991.

Kirban, Salem. *Guide to Survival*. Wheaton, Ill.: Tyndale House Publishers, 1968.

Lindsey, Hal. *The Late Great Planet Earth*. Grand Rapids: Zondervan Publishing House, 1971.

Lowery, T.L. *The End of the World*. Cleveland, Tenn.: Lowery Publications, 1969.

McMillen, S.I. *Discern These Times*. Old Tappan, N.J.: Fleming H. Revell Co., 1971.

Olson, Arnold. *Inside Jerusalem*. Glendale, Calif.: Regal Books, 1968.

Pentecost, J. Dwight. *Things to Come*. Grand Rapids: Zondervan Publishing House, 1964.

Poland, Larry W. *The Coming Persecution*. San Bernardino, Calif.: Here's Life Publishers, 1990.

Ryrie, Charles C. *The Bible and Tomorrow's News*. Wheaton, Ill.: Scripture Press Publications, Inc., 1969.

Smith, Oswald J. *Prophecy—What Lies Ahead?* London: Marshall, Morgan & Scott, 1967.

Smith, Wilbur M. *You Can Know the Future*. Glendale, Calif.: Regal Books, 1971.

Stedman, Ray C. *What on Earth's Going to Happen?* Glendale, Calif.: Regal Books, 1970.

Stevenson, William. *Strike Zion!* New York: Bantam Books, Inc., 1967.

Strauss, Lehman. *God's Plan for the Future*. Grand Rapids: Zondervan Publishing House, 1965.

Strauss, Lehman. *The Prophecies of Daniel*. Neptune, N.J.: Loizeaux Brothers, 1969.

Synan, J.A. *The Shape of Things to Come*. Franklin Springs, Ga.: Advocate Press, 1969.

Talbot, Louis T. *God's Plan of the Ages*. Grand Rapids: William B. Eerdmans Publishing Co., 1946.

Walvoord, John F. *Armageddon, Oil, and the Middle East Crisis*. Grand Rapids: Zondervan Publishing House, 1990.

Walvoord, John F. *Daniel, The Key to Prophetic Revelation*. Chicago: Moody Press, 1971.

Walvoord, John F. *The Revelation of Jesus Christ*. Chicago: Moody Press, 1966.

White, John Wesley. *Re-entry*. Grand Rapids: Zondervan Publishing House, 1970.